EXCITEMENT FOR MUDRUNNER

"While people often talk about sacrificing for Jesus or going to "the ends of the earth," Charlie has actually done it, carrying the Gospel into some of the most remote or spiritually dark places in the world. His real-life stories of victory, danger and struggle in the mission field will give you chills and leave you praising our Faithful Father. I pray that *Mudrunner* will challenge each reader to dig deeper into God's Word and develop a burden to share the hope of Jesus near and far."

Will Graham
Evangelist and Vice President,
Billy Graham Evangelistic Association
Executive Director, Billy Graham Training Center at The Cove
Author, *Redeemed: Devotions for the Longing Soul*

"Charlie Marquis is living out Paul's exhortation to 'never be lacking in zeal, but keep your spiritual fervor, serving the Lord.' Reading *Mudrunner* will inspire you to do the same. Charlie's calling is taking him to hard places where the gospel isn't available. But the principles remind us a life of total abandon is for every

Jesus follower, regardless of where God has positioned you. Open the pages of this book, and open your heart to what God has for you, no matter the cost."

Steve Moore
President, nexleader
Author, *The Top 10 Leadership Conversations in the Bible: Practical Insights from Extensive Research on Over 1,000 Biblical Leaders*
Former President and CEO, Missio Nexus

"Amazing journey of how God is using people like you and me to radically advance His kingdom and reach the lost. *Mudrunner* takes you from the comfort of your church to the front lines of evangelism in some of the toughest places and makes you question, 'Could I go and make disciples of all nations?' There is no Plan B; we, the Church, *are* God's plan to reach the lost, feed the hungry, and comfort the sick. *Mudrunner* shows us that God can and will use ordinary people like us in mighty ways if we just answer the call and step out boldly in faith."

Lance Putnam
Founder and Host, Legacy Dads Podcast / Ministry

"Charlie is a fireball for Jesus. Charlie's global stories of following Jesus anywhere to do anything are bound to stir your soul and leave you challenged. But look out! His love for Jesus and go-get-it spirit may ignite a fire in you to abandon your comfort zone as well."

"Biz"
Founder, Unusual Soldiers
Author, *Dangerous: Engaging the People and Places No One Else Will*

"Get ready for the ultimate off-road ministry experience that puts missions back in the adventure business. *Mudrunner* is an exciting reminder that preaching the gospel is not a sterile religious obligation but a grueling race in some of the darkest regions on Earth. When we think of mud runs, we often think of Tough Mudders, Spartan Races, Warrior Dashes, and Rugged Maniacs, but Charlie Marquis uses vivid testimonies from around the world to paint a picture of the ultimate mud run: the mission field.

These stories inspire and compel Christians to do something that has been lost in modern ministry: find joy in suffering. The appeal to take the gospel message to the most impoverished areas on Earth is an extreme command from Jesus to His followers and is not for the faint of heart. Throughout the pages of this book, *Mudrunner* reminds us again and again that the Great Commission will not be fulfilled by those who seek comfort and riches, but will only be accomplished by those who 'embrace the suck.' As someone who thoroughly enjoys a good mission story and strongly believes that we must do everything possible to accomplish the Great Commission in our lifetime—I highly recommend this book."

Eugene Bach
Trouble-Maker-In-Chief, Back to Jerusalem
Coauthor, *The Underground Church*
Coauthor, *Leaving Buddha: A Tibetan Monk's Encounter with the Living God*
Author, *China and End-Time Prophecy: How God Is Using the Red Dragon to Fulfill His Ultimate Purposes*

"*Mudrunner* is a global journey filled with tales of missionary grit and holy determination. Charlie guides you from Denver's streets to East Africa's jungles, from Buddhist temples in the Himalayas to tribal villages in Southeast Asia. He peppers the narrative with parabolic teaching, provoking the reader to persist in faith's marathon. Charlie describes Jesus as the ultimate mudrunner: intent to accomplish His Father's will in the face of life's obstacles. *Mudrunner* inspires you to run with endurance the race set before you, knowing that with every step you take, you're following in Jesus' footsteps."

David Joannes
Founder, Within Reach Global
Author, *The Mind of a Missionary: What Global Kingdom Workers Tell Us About Thriving on Mission Today*

"Charlie clearly loves adventure! This book is so him. He's following hard after Jesus and has his eyes on the ends of the earth. He wants the hard places, the forgotten people, the least reached. He wants to reach people for Jesus who are caught in Satan's grip in the strongholds of Buddhism, Hinduism, and Islam. His book is full of unforgettable stories going way 'off-road' to reach them. While I'm sixty-three, Charlie's book makes me want to go with him as a mudrunner to the ends of the earth. I believe God wants to use Charlie to inspire an entire generation to radically lay down their lives and follow Jesus! I'm praying God uses this book to grab your heart and turn you into one of these mudrunners too!"

Diane Brask
Executive Director, Global Seed Planters

"*Mudrunner* has a similar feel to David Platt's stories and writing. It is a book that needs to be picked up cautiously because it will challenge you to your core. Charlie writes from his experiences serving overseas and the lessons he learned along the way. Each chapter reveals what it means to surrender and say YES to Jesus and to keep saying YES. This book communicates clearly that it is not easy to engage in the mission of God, but it is the very purpose for which we were created."

Mick Veach
Lead Pastor, Kentwood Community Church, Kentwood, MI
Founder, Mosaic Midtown Church of Detroit
Former full-time missionary among the unreached

"For the past two decades I have lived a life surrendered to the Great Commission. Yet through *Mudrunner*, I have been inspired, challenged, and faced with the brutal reality that I can always do more to advance God's kingdom. The true stories of transformed lives, redeemed tribes, and opposition overcome have left me marked and ready to take on a new adventure for God. Charlie makes it clear: simple obedience is the first step toward living a radical life for Jesus. After reading this book, you will be ready to pray, 'What next, Lord?' and then I hope you pursue it!"

Jason Holland
President, Joshua Nations

"Charlie is well acquainted with the mission of advancing the kingdom of God, and has gotten down and dirty in taking the gospel message to the nations. Charlie fearlessly proclaims King Jesus wherever the Spirit leads him, and this book is filled with inspiring stories of those adventures. I believe you will be inspired and challenged to fearless obedience to God and His Great Commission, wherever you are and whatever your station."

John Vermilya
Lead Pastor, The Tabernacle Church, Buckley, MI

"*Mudrunner* is a witness to the continuing work of God in this world. Charlie inspires us all to see our world with the kingdom eyes of Jesus."

Robert Gelinas
Lead Pastor, Colorado Community Church
Author, *Discipled by Jesus: Your Ongoing Invitation to Follow Jesus*

"*Mudrunner* is not a book of stories. Rather, found in these pages you will find an invitation into a story that God is writing and calling you into. You will no doubt find yourself greatly inspired to enter the great race of making the name of Jesus known in and through your life—as you do, you just might find that you were born to run in the mud."

Nirup Alphonse
Lead Pastor, LifeGate Church Denver

"If you care about Jesus' heart cry for more kingdom laborers, *Mudrunner* is a must read! Be forewarned, however: you can't read this book and keep your 'beautiful feet' (Romans 10:15) neat and tidy! Mud-running feet get dirty, dusty, even mud-caked. Why? Because willing hearts (and able feet) move at the impulse of God's love to engage mud puddles of human need where Jesus' truth, love, and works need delivered. No wonder in a room full of 'beautiful' dirty feet, Jesus tenderly stooped, held, and washed feet about to travel toward unreached places and people. Jesus treasured their mud-running delivery potential, as He does yours.

Charlie's feet—employed, directed, and empowered by Jesus—have experienced numerous mud-running missions to destinations few dare to go. Charlie's unusual adventures, exciting God stories, and hands-on mud-running tips challenge, equip, and inspire us all to live fearlessly for the kingdom cause. As you read and engage *Mudrunner*, be prepared for God to ignite a fire in your heart, set your feet to running, and lead you straight into some exceptional God-led mud-puddle runs of your own!"

Dwight Robertson
Founding President and CEO, FORGE: Kingdom Building
Ministries
International Speaker and Author, *You Are God's Plan A, and There
Is No Plan B*; *Forged by Fire: Making Intimacy with God Your
Greatest Gift*; and *Is God Waiting for a Date with You?*

"Every generation, God raises up voices that pierce through the noise of complacency and excuses to generate a clear signal that calls us to His mission. If you're reading this book, you're receiving the signal. *Mudrunner* reminds me of Loren Cunningham's conviction and writing, and is a story you must hear because it will embolden, challenge, and confirm so many parts of your own story. Whether you're a paper pusher, digital diver, crowd watcher, or solitude seeker, there is a mudrunner within you! Don't only enjoy this book—get lost in the story and find yourself in between the lines. Happy running!"

Fred Lynch
Communicator, Author, Creative, FredLynch.org

"Drawing on years of life experiences, both struggles and triumphs, *Mudrunner* serves as an inspirational testimony to the work the Lord can do through those who faithfully seek to serve as His instruments. Through sharing firsthand experiences, supplemented with theological wisdom, *Mudrunner* takes readers on a journey to many remote and isolated places throughout the world while exposing the truth of spiritual battles and warfare in the lives of everyday people. Whether you are a scientist or construction worker, a teacher or business leader, this book demonstrates that you are not simply what you do for a living. Rather, we are all defined by how passionately and endlessly we commit ourselves to the pursuit of serving God through the advancement of His kingdom."

"John Smith"
Undercover Soldier Fighting Human Trafficking

MUDRUNNER

ADVANCING THE KINGDOM—NO MATTER THE PEOPLE, THE PLACE, OR THE COST

CHARLIE MARQUIS

ILLUMIFY
MEDIA.COM

Paperback ISBN: 978-1-947360-96-9
eBook ISBN: 978-1-947360-97-6

Typeset by Jennifer Clark
Cover design by Debbie Lewis

Printed in the United States of America

DEDICATION

People have been asking me for years to write down the stories of all I have witnessed God do around the world. I knew God wanted me to share these stories; the question has always been when and how? On a plane in Asia, the vision and plan for this book clearly unfolded as God revealed to me,
"Charlie, now is the time."

For those who have prayed for and supported the vision:
these are your God stories.

For Grandpa Peter:
I finally understood what you wanted to hear from my very first mission trip, not just the "good" we did, but the Jesus stories. Here they are!

For Onwas:
You are one of the first from your tribe to now dance before the throne of God for all of eternity.

For my wife and family:
Thank you for your sacrifice as you embrace the call of God,
continuing to send me out time and time again.
Hold onto these frontline Jesus stories,
made possible because of your sacrifice.

For the mudrunners
who give their lives day in and day out for the sake of God's kingdom:
This book is not only written for you but by you.

CONTENTS

THE STARTING LINE: MUD RUNS

"Are you sure it's a good idea to continue?" Nathan asked.

The sun was setting, and darkness would soon surround us.

"Yes, let's keep going. I don't want to waste any more time on this journey." I noted that our motorcycles had adequate headlights and, although night was upon us, the trip shouldn't take too long. "We should be fine," I said before driving off to lead the way.

Not long after, I ate my own words as several of our motorcycles broke down and we found ourselves stranded in the dark along a slick mud road on the side of a mountain.

My friend and ministry partner, Nathan, along with myself and several nationals were traveling to a remote Himalayan village to spend time training believers to reach the unreached. But the muddy mountains were going to delay our mission a bit longer.

We somehow found a small guesthouse along the side of the road and managed to walk our motorcycles there. The owners invited us in. Ducking our heads, we entered their modest living space. The hosts offered us tea while they continued preparing the evening meal, rice and curry.

As we sipped our tea and peered into the fire heating the clay oven, we were grateful for this unexpected stop. We needed rest and God provided it. After dinner, we laid down on the beds they provided. Unlike the mud and the mountain, the hard-surfaced beds posed no obstacle for us in immediately falling to sleep.

The next morning, our journey began with pouring rain. The target village was still quite a distance away. The locals told us about a small town about a mile away where we might catch a four-by-four mountain taxi that regularly drove to the region we were traveling to. Because my motorcycle was the only one that hadn't broken down, I drove Nathan to the small town. Nathan hopped off to wait with the taxi while I rode back to collect the others.

I drove back to where we had been lodging as quickly as I could. I parked the motorcycle and gathered my two Himalayan friends, Aliza and Aadesh. We grabbed our backpacks and started walking.

When we arrived, neither Nathan nor the taxi were anywhere to be found. The rain continued pouring. Communicating with Nathan wasn't possible. I was left to assume Nathan made his way to our destination for reasons he alone knew.

For hours we trekked in the pouring rain, slipping and sliding in thick, sloppy mud. We were soaked from head to toe. I confess that along the way I had a few disparaging thoughts: *Must be nice, Nathan! You get the quick, dry ride and we get a sopping-wet hike!*

Determined, we continued forging forward—step by step and, at times, inch by inch. I prayed, *Lord, I hope you make our time in this village worth it.*

Immediately the Lord replied with this thought: *"Do you believe I am worthy of this, Charlie?"*

Forgive me, Lord. Yes, of course you are worthy! I will consider this pure joy no matter the outcome. It is worth it because you are worthy of it!

After hiking for much of the day, we made it to the village. And God worked mightily among the believers there.

While I would never have chosen that rain-soaked, mud-laden experience on my own, the temporary hardship was well worth it that day. The prolonged obstacle-filled journey reminded me of those who encounter mud-filled adventures, not because they must but because they can. There are people who actually *choose* to "suffer" through mud-filled adventures known as *mud runs*—and all in the name of fun!

Mud runs are mud-filled obstacle course races. There are numerous variations and names: Tough Mudder, Spartan Race, Warrior Dash, and Rugged Maniacs, just to name a few. These races are not for the faint of heart. They require great endurance, eyes-on-the-prize tenacity, and at times, a gritting of the teeth. They don't draw the "one-and-done" kind of people. Rather, a "Tough Mudder is no ordinary mud run," as one expert sees it; "it's a way of life." Tough Mudder events require what I like to call *mudrunners*. Though they may be drenched in mud from head to toe, mudrunners engage any obstacle to push forward, fighting hard to cross the finish line no matter what it takes. Mudrunners radiate the "It's hard, but it's worth it" mentality. I believe God is looking for more mudrunners for His kingdom cause.

I am drawn to the words of Paul the apostle who wrote, "I consider my life worth nothing to me; my only aim is to finish the race and complete the task the Lord Jesus has given me—the task of testifying to the good news of God's grace" (Acts 20:24 NIV). Not only did Paul begin the race; he victoriously crossed the finish line. But it was surely no easy feat.

Paul fought hard to run his race, describing it this way: "For I am already being poured out as a drink offering . . . I have fought the good fight, I have finished the race, I have kept the faith" (2 Timothy 4:6–7 ESV).

Paul uses a graphic picture to summarize his mudrunner lifestyle: "a drink offering." As a sacrifice to God, Jews poured *drink offerings* into the fire of the altar to offer a representation of themselves to God. Drink offerings were ultimately fulfilled in Jesus pouring out his life and spilling His blood on the cross, the blood of the new covenant. While the blood of Jesus fulfilled the need for literal drink offerings to be given, Jesus calls us to offer our lives to God—to die daily to our own pleasures and desires in order to live for something much greater: God's kingdom cause.

Paul continually poured out his life, offensively advancing God's kingdom wherever he stepped foot, which proved to be far tougher than any mud run out there.

Paul embraced extreme obstacles and challenges for the sake of this Kingdom "Tough Mudder": often exposed to death; beaten with rods three times; attacked with rocks; shipwrecked three times; afloat for a day and night in the open sea; constantly on the move; in danger from rivers, bandits, false believers, Jews, and Gentiles; in danger in the city, in the country, and at sea; often without sleep, without food, and thirsty; consistently imprisoned, cold, and naked; and severely flogged five separate times. Each flogging consisted of thirty-nine lashes from a whip with nine leather straps containing fragments of barbed metal balls and sharp bones designed to sink into the skin and rip it to shreds (2 Corinthians 11:23–27).

Clearly, "charging into the fire" for God's kingdom cause was more important to Paul than his own comfort—and even his own life. He picked up the shoes of a mudrunner, ran his race, and through his determination, finished well.

Jesus is still looking for mudrunners who will advance His kingdom as a way of life. This kingdom needs lifestyle mudrunners willing to give their unreserved yes when asking, "Is God's kingdom cause truly worth any cost to my life? And do I really believe Jesus is worthy of it all?"

God first invited me into the race when He called me to itinerant ministry—traveling from place to place, both in my country and around the globe, to preach the message of Jesus anywhere and everywhere to crowds large and small, and to ultimately propagate a movement of kingdom laborers, otherwise known as mudrunners.

When I first stepped out in faith, I often felt inadequate and wondered how I could best run the race God had placed in front of me.

Through it all, God has been faithful. The unique path God set for me has led to numerous ventures throughout all sorts of countries around the world. I have seen great victories and equally made plenty of mistakes. Running the race has brought some of the best days of my life and included some of the worst. The question remains: has it been worth it? My answer undeniably stands: absolutely!

This lifestyle of faith, this mudrunner kingdom adventure, isn't for me alone. It's meant for you too! All it requires is a willingness to say yes to whatever God asks, whenever He asks it.

I envision an army of mudrunners for God's kingdom—gathering at the starting line, running their race—and all faithfully crossing the finish line in victory, passionately advancing God's kingdom anywhere and everywhere they go. Will you be one of them?

I hope you see yourself among them. I hope you take up the challenge to become a mudrunner and run your race for the glory of God.

It won't be easy. Tough times are ahead. Mud, hardship, and even persecution may await you. In the midst of it all, I promise you: running for the cause of Christ is worth it because He is worthy of it!

As you continue through this book, I pray that chapter by chapter Jesus further equips you to join Him in His Kingdom cause. May you become a mudrunner who declares with reckless abandon, "It's hard, but it's worth it!"

ONE

THE GATES OF HELL

WHAT BETTER PLACE TO start the mudrunner journey than hell itself!

I finally made it to South Asia, despite unprecedented challenges. My heart pounded with exhilaration for the Jesus adventure awaiting us.

"Hey, Arpan," I said to my friend and ministry colleague, "what do you think about going to an unreached region and visiting a Hindu temple?"

"Yes, let's go!" he replied.

We hopped in Arpan's car. After several hours of driving, we pulled up to a white temple with stunning architecture. We prayerfully walked into the temple courtyard, planning to keep our eyes open for kingdom opportunity and share about Jesus if we could find a way to do so.

Arpan and I walked to the end of the courtyard and approached the "holy place" where the priests sat in front of their gods, which were lifeless idols crafted by the hands of mere men. These priests wore white sashes that were wrapped over one shoulder and folded around their waists like a skirt. Paint covered their wrinkled faces, and a red dot marked their foreheads, acting as their "third eye."

We approached the priest on the left. I couldn't help but look behind him to the temple and the "god" it enshrined. What I saw behind the priest reminded me of the stark reality he might face in eternity. As incense burned, smoke surrounded the idol and filled the temple. The blue-skinned idol stood lifelessly staring at me. With its tongue stuck out, the idol was holding a cutoff head, dripping blood. It wreaked of chaos and surely resembled some sort of hell.

I couldn't help but think about the irony—that while looking for peace, blessing, and goodness, Hindus worship some of the most disturbing, violent, and evil-looking creatures known to mankind. *Surely they must be searching for something more than this!* I thought.

Arpan and I struck up a conversation with the priest to see if it might lead to a conversation about Jesus.

As the three of us were talking, an old man hobbled into the temple area. He slowly walked toward the idols, laid down his sacrifice, and then made his way to where we were standing. Falling on his face before the priest, he kissed the priest's feet several times. With tears in his eyes, he petitioned the priest. "Bless me, bless me, bless me!" the man cried out in a loud voice.

Intense burden filled my heart. I longed to tell this man about the God whose burden is light, the God who could take all his afflictions and truly bless him. I turned toward Arpan and said, "My heart is burdened for this man. I think we need to talk with him."

"Yes," agreed Arpan, "I'm feeling the same way."

"Okay, let's go talk with him." By the time I finished muttering this sentence to Arpan, I looked around and the old man had somehow already gotten up and hobbled back to the entrance. We quickly pursued him out of the gates and into the street.

"Namaste!" I greeted him.

The man yelled a few words back at me that I didn't understand.

Arpan translated. "He is asking what you said."

The man was half deaf, loudly shouting and repeating himself just to understand a simple greeting.

I looked around the busy street. *Well, this could be interesting. We may have to yell back and forth in this place just to have a conversation. And since sharing the gospel is illegal here, we might stir up all sorts of trouble on this packed public street!*

We tried to continue conversing, but the old man staggered off. Our hope of conversation crumbled.

Meanwhile, a young man doggedly followed us on a bike and repeatedly called out to me, "Hey, where you from?" in broken English.

I heard him, but I intentionally chose to ignore him as Arpan and I continued attempting to engage the elderly man. Knowing it's rarely wise to draw attention to yourself in a foreign land or to respond to a random stranger's beckoning, my plan was to continue ignoring him.

But his persistence finally got to me. I turned back and said, "Hey bro, I am from USA. How are you?"

"I am fine, thank you," he replied, "And how are you?" His phrasing mimicked the typical English response taught by many schools around the globe.

"I am doing well. My name is Charlie. What is your name?"

"My name is Sakar," he responded.

We were still standing outside the temple gates, and I sensed that the potential of conversation with the old man had actually led us to this new one.

I felt compelled to inquire, "Sakar, what is your dream? What do you want to do with your life?"

"I want to join my country's military," he confidently proclaimed.

"Really? I almost joined the military in my country."

"What stopped you?" Sakar inquired. "Why didn't you join?"

"Well, I worked very hard and actually was about to achieve

my goal! In fact, the military awarded me with a full-ride scholarship and incredible leadership opportunity. But something interesting happened before I joined. One day, as I was spending time
with God and praying, He asked me to give up my military dream
and put Him first in my life. He then asked me to travel around
the world and tell other people about Him! In the process, I have
discovered that God satisfies far more than any dream or desire we
could ever have! This God's name is Jesus. He changed my life. He
can actually interact with us and we can have a true relationship
with Him. You can have a relationship with this God, Jesus, too."

Sakar intently listened.

Arpan added, "It's true, Sakar. You do not have to worship
God in a temple. He can live inside of you and you can worship
Him anywhere."

"Sakar," I asked, "do you normally worship in this temple?"

"Yes, I always come here to worship."

"You can have a relationship with the one true living God
because Jesus came and died as a sacrifice for all our sins which
separate us from the presence of God. Jesus rose from the dead and
is alive today. You do not have to give sacrifices here to please God.
You simply have to believe in Jesus and follow Him, no longer
worshiping any other gods. Do you want to believe in Jesus?"

"Yes, I really do want to believe in Jesus," Sakar said with
excitement.

"Okay, you can pray now and tell Jesus that you believe in
Him and all He has done for you, and that you want to begin a
relationship with Him. It can be in your own words."

Sakar began praying. Surprisingly, he began confessing his sins
to God out loud, right there in the street! It was evident Jesus was
taking ahold of his heart.

Sakar finished praying. He was made alive in Christ in that
very moment! We exchanged contact information and went our
separate ways. Arpan and I later created a local follow-up plan for
Sakar to grow in the faith. God's kingdom had advanced—and of
all places, just outside a Hindu temple!

This wasn't the first time God had ever done such a thing. The

Gospel writer Matthew tells about a time Jesus took his disciples to a place where heavy spiritual darkness hovered (Matthew 16). Jesus led his disciples to Caesarea Philippi, a well-known center of idol worship. It was home to a number of pagan temples, nestled at the base of a massive cliff that loomed over the edge of the city. Worshippers of the Emperor Caesar as well as gods named Baal and Pan often traveled to these temples to make sacrifices. Unspeakable acts such as bestiality with goats became encouraged forms of worship. These worshippers believed that spirits roamed back and forth from the realm of the dead through the waterway in the cliff. They called that opening "the Gates of Hades" or "the Gates of Hell." Sound familiar? (Matthew 16:18).

I've often wondered what the disciples personally experienced when they stepped foot in places like "the Gates of Hell." On my own expeditions of venturing into temples, places of spirit and ancestor worship, brothels, red-light districts, villages without a single believer, mosques, and regions of violent persecution, I have experienced palpable spiritual darkness. Walking into some of these places has felt like walking into a bubble of demonic Jell-O.

I once walked into some of this thick Jell-O when I walked into a "special holy room" where I witnessed locals bowing down to two embalmed dead bodies. One by one, they took turns bowing down to the left side, then at the feet, and then at the right side of each of these bodies, these "gods" who were the two former leaders of this Asian Communist country. I felt like I could taste the spiritual darkness. From head to toe, my entire body experienced a distinct heaviness and oppression that hovered over the room.

On another occasion, I walked into a Muslim Somalian region and felt soul-shaking chaos. A sense of anxiety skyrocketed. I couldn't explain it, but the chaos was limited only to that Somali region.

As I have visited various mosques all over the world, they all share a common spirit, that of deception. Buddhist monasteries I've entered around the world also seem to share a unified yet unique "spiritual air" inside them. In some of these places, evil feels thick and weighty. It's as if you can almost see specific dark messengers sent by Satan to keep entire people groups in darkness, deception, and oppression.

While the darkness may be vivid, we do not have to be afraid to step foot in such places, because Jesus Himself protects us. I have certainly learned this incredible reality. Not only can we *defensively* fight the spiritual battle as the enemy slings mud our way, but we can fight *offensively*, grabbing hold of the sword of the Spirit and venturing to take His Word into spiritually dark places. I, for one, am often eager to do so!

Jesus didn't run in fear from these spiritually dark, despised, and sin-soiled places. Jesus didn't try to avoid them. Jesus did not seem fazed. In fact, "the Gates of Hell" was the exact place Jesus took his disciples to reveal and proclaim that He was the Messiah.

Jesus was not proclaimed as the Messiah in Jerusalem, the central city of Judaism. Jesus was not proclaimed as the Messiah in a synagogue or religious gathering place. No, Jesus was proclaimed as the Messiah by Peter in one of the spiritually darkest places of the day where few Jews would dare to step foot.

And as if that was not enough, Jesus proclaimed, "On this rock I will build my church and the gates of hell shall not prevail against it" (Matthew 16:18 ESV). It is most commonly taught that Peter's proclamation of faith was the rock upon which Jesus would build His Church. While Jesus did begin building His Church on Peter's proclamation of faith in that moment, I believe there is more to the story. I believe Jesus wanted His disciples to understand that He could build His Church anywhere, even in the most unimaginably dark places, places like the rock cliff of Caesarea Philippi. As His followers, we can proclaim the kingship of Jesus Christ in any place of spiritual darkness, and He will build His Church; and nothing will overcome it—not the pagan cliff of Caesarea Philippi nor any place of utter darkness in our day and time.

Jesus' proclamation is not a *defensive* statement but an *offensive* one. Jesus wasn't describing the Church hiding out in a fortress while hell attacks. Rather, Jesus was painting a picture of the

Church on the move, advancing—knocking down the gates of hell and infiltrating the darkness! These are the kinds of doors that God is calling us to knock down, as tough as the mission may be and regardless the size of the obstacles that lay in our path.

When Jesus ascended to heaven, His disciples went into *all* the earth—even to the darkest places—and Jesus began building His Church. It began then. It continues to this day.

So, as followers of Jesus, how should we approach spiritual darkness? What should we do?

I no longer view places of darkness as places to run from or avoid. I now see spiritually dark places as opportunities to advance God's kingdom and join Jesus in His cause for the world. It truly is the darkness that most desperately needs the light.

Jesus has always wanted to engage the spiritually dirty and muddy places. His plan is to do so through mudrunners like you and me. As you engage the dark and muddy places, you might just see Jesus embraced as the Messiah, the Savior, among those who need Him most! In fact, He has even promised that in those places He will build His Church. Are you ready to join His offensive charge into the darkness?

Now What?

- What are some of the spiritually dark places you've seen in your everyday life?
- How do you think Jesus might want to advance His kingdom there?
- Rather than run from them, how can you engage those places with the light of Christ?

TWO

WHY WE RUN

I AM CURRENTLY SITTING with a cup of chai tea and my laptop in Downtown Denver. On the drive here I passed several homeless guys holding cardboard signs as they stared into oblivion, waiting and hoping that their lives might change. Or maybe simply waiting and hoping they will find enough food and warmth to make it through the night.

I am reminded of a time I saw a homeless man with a sign that read NEED SHOES.

Approaching the man, I said, "I am Charlie. What's your name?"

"I am Willis."

A large man, Willis towered over me. Being a whopping five feet five inches tall myself, it struck me that we must have looked like David and Goliath. I said, "Willis, I don't think my shoes will fit you. But I want to ask you something: Do you know anything about Jesus?"

Without warning, Willis was screaming. Worse yet, he was screaming at me. "I hate you Christians!" he shouted. "Get out of my face! Go away before I beat you!!"

While this probably wasn't the wisest idea, I thought, *Why not stick around for a few more minutes and see if the conversation can go any further?*

It didn't.

As I walked away, Willis shouted an accusation I will never forget: "You Christians are always walking by me, but you don't even look at me."

That statement hit me hard. As I thought about it through the rest of the day, it began sinking deeply into my heart. The Lord began to convict me as I wondered, *How many people have I passed by without really seeing? How many people have I ignored or never even noticed? How many people have I simply not cared about?*

Jesus didn't just "pass on by" people like Willis. No, Jesus *saw* each person. He took note of them. He observed where they were and moved in closer to engage them. Matthew 9:36 says, "When [Jesus] *saw* the crowds, he had compassion for them" (ESV, italics mine).

I haven't always seen the heartfelt needs of people like Jesus does. And when I do catch a glimpse of the profound needs around me, it's so overwhelming. It's so easy to get paralyzed and wonder, *What can I even do?*

Have you ever felt overwhelmed by the needs around you?

God has a unique race for you that will uniquely engage the needs of the world around you. It's a race that involves loving Him with everything you've got and radically loving the people around you, including people like Willis.

In fact, the Bible gives us this life-changing invitation: "Let us run . . . the race that is set before us" (Hebrews 12:1 ESV). This is something that anyone and everyone *can* do and is invited to do. The sad reality, however, is that many people miss out on this race. Far too many Christians are living on the sidelines, never making it to the starting line, and never running the race set before them. Far too many never take up the true cause of Christ: to love Him with everything, to love others as more important than self, and to make disciples of all nations.

Even more tragic is the fact that, when we don't say "yes"— when we don't accept the invitation and run the race that God has called us to run—other people suffer. There are people, like Willis, who have no idea God is inviting them to run their own unique race. And they never will if you and I don't step up to the starting line and run our race with all we've got.

Maybe you've made it to the track but have been putting off approaching the starting line and beginning the race. I certainly waited too long to jump into the action. But once I did, it was surely worth it! The adrenaline rush, the thrill, and the pure joy of the cause was immeasurable. I never knew the race could be such an exciting adventure! No one ever told me. Or more likely, they did tell me, but I was too thick-skulled for it to sink in. Whatever the case, now that I've begun the race, there is no looking back!

One day I found myself in one of the most unreached, restricted, and dangerous countries in the world for followers of Jesus. As I sat on a bus and peered out the window, I saw what you might expect to witness in third world nations: impoverished farmers in small villages, hungry children, and people digging water out of ditches, all in between somewhat developed cities with people scurrying to and fro.

As I continued to watch, I began taking note of the faces of all the people we passed. Over and over I saw dull eyes, downcast expressions, countenances of intense darkness. I saw lost, broken, helpless, and hopeless people in desperate need of something more than they had been given.

Living in a country that strictly outlawed access to the message of Jesus, every single one of them, I realized, had probably never heard the gospel, likely never would, and couldn't hear it even if they wanted to!

As that reality sunk in, I began to feel burdened and even sick to my stomach. As I prayed, a gut-wrenching burden for the people emerged.

I was immediately reminded of Matthew 9:36: "When Jesus saw the crowds, he had compassion on them, because they were harassed and helpless, like sheep without a shepherd" (NIV). That's what I was witnessing: harassed and helpless sheep without a shepherd, people who had no understanding of the compassion of Jesus for them.

Jesus did not simply feel bad for the people. The word *compassion* in the Scriptures literally means "to be moved as to one's bowels." Jesus had a gut-wrenching burden for the people. And on that day, I experienced Jesus' gut-wrenching compassion, His burden for others, in a new way.

Have you ever wondered how Jesus feels about the hopeless? Maybe the word *hopeless* even describes you, or those you encounter in your daily life, or the rest of the world. The hopeless for whom Jesus feels gut-wrenching compassion includes people in your family, people in your workplace, random acquaintances, and even people groups that you've never heard of living halfway around the globe!

The good news is that the deep compassion of Jesus does not leave any one of us hopeless and abandoned, wandering and lost with no way out.

How do I know this?

Because Jesus looked at his disciples and said, "The harvest is plentiful, but the laborers are few; therefore pray earnestly to the Lord of the harvest to send out laborers into his harvest" (Matthew 9:37–38 ESV).

In just one phrase Jesus identified both the world's greatest need and the greatest solution to that need. More laborers. That was His answer. That *is* His answer. Who will love the struggling neighbors down the street? Who will care for that depressed high school student across the classroom? Who will drill water wells for those who are diseased due to bad water? Who will rescue those who have been trafficked and enslaved? Who will fight for the oppressed? Who will provide sustainable solutions for the starving? Who will bring relief to victims of natural disasters? Who will proclaim the path of eternal peace and hope? Laborers. Laborers who bring the good news of everything Jesus offers are the solution to the needs we see all around us. Jesus is the one hope and singular answer to all of these issues, and laborers are those who house this living Jesus, bringing Him up close to the world around them. Kingdom laborers are the *only* solution!

Back in that restricted Asian country, peering out the windows of the bus and experiencing this gut-wrenching burden for the harassed and helpless before me, I prayed, *Lord, who will go? Who will share the message of the gospel with them? God, somehow, some-way, send more laborers to this place!*

Whenever I hear the word *laborer,* I envision those who *go,* those being *sent out.* I envision laborers as those who engage the dirt and the mud of the fields for the sake of the crop. They do what must be done. They exhibit perseverance and resilience. I do not believe Jesus' laborers are like those who jog nice short-distance races on dry pavement. Laboring for God's kingdom looks a lot more like an intense, long-distance mud run. I really believe that those who labor for God's kingdom truly are *mudrunners.*

I am always amazed to witness those who live as mudrunners, day in and day out.

Like my friend Mary. Mary is a Hadzabe tribal woman who lives in a mud-brick house in a small village town in East Africa. The Hadzabe (or Hadza) are a nomadic tribe of people who speak an isolated click language, live in dome grass huts, and hunt with poison bows and arrows. They traditionally worship the sun in the sky and pray to ancestral spirits. Before 2014 they had no church, no Bible, and no discipleship in their language. Talk about a people in great need!

Mary's ordinary yet radical story of Jesus began on my second journey to visit the Hadzabe people. My friend Nathan and I ventured into the bush (otherwise known as the East African jungle) with a vision to spark a disciple-making movement among this unreached tribe. Mary was the only Hadzabe person who knew English and could translate for us, so we began a relation-ship. When we met her, she did not yet have a relationship with the living Jesus.

As we began the ministry to the Hadzabe, Mary became inti-mately acquainted with every message we preached. In fact, she translated every word! I couldn't help but think that what we were teaching and preaching would begin to sink into her heart.

One day I asked, "Mary, are you ready to give your own life to Jesus?"

She replied, "No, not yet."

A few days later and somewhat out of nowhere, Mary looked at me and said, "Charlie, I'm ready. I want to give my life to Jesus today. Let's pray tonight."

That night we came around a campfire in the middle of the bush and Mary gave her life to Jesus. We had no idea that the spark ignited in her would soon become a raging wildfire!

A week later I asked Mary, "Since you have committed your life to Jesus, have you heard Him speak anything to you? Do you feel different in any way?"

She replied, "Yes. I now have hope in my heart, and I hear God saying to me, 'Do not be afraid of the difficulty, I will be with you.'"

Mary had approached the starting line, ready to surge forward. Her race was beginning!

It wasn't long before Mary realized that God had designed a unique race for her, desiring to work through her life for His kingdom purposes. One day Mary came to me and said, "Last night when I went to bed, I was praying for the Hadzabe, for the gospel to go out to all of them. I had a dream and God spoke to me. He said, 'Mary, begin teaching at the village led by Mambos.'"

The very next week Mary began teaching Hadzabe tribals in Mambos's village, an unreached village near her home. How did she begin? Mary shared the Word of God with the villagers for an entire day! And her ministry has only expanded from there.

I have been amazed by Mary's compassion for her people. She doesn't leave the compassion to Jesus. She carries it with her as she draws near to those in great need. Although she has lived as a poor single mother of two, it is not uncommon to find Mary feeding the hungry with her small amounts of food, caring for drunks (no matter what hour of the night they show up yelling, "Mary! Mary! Are you there?! Are you awake?!"), and sharing stories of Jesus with those who have never heard. She does not cease to love the way Jesus loves, utilizing the everyday tools that God has given her.

Mary has decided that broken lives are worth it. She's committed to seeing people as Jesus sees them. She's willing to overcome any obstacle that comes her way, doing whatever it takes to see more people meet the living Jesus.

God brought hope to Mary. Now He is bringing hope *through* Mary. She has picked up her running shoes and become one of God's mudrunners!

God isn't simply looking for more pastors, ministry leaders, or seminary graduates. He's looking for more ordinary people to become everyday mudrunners. He's wanting to enlist willing runners who will love God, love others, and make disciples in ways that utilize their unique personality, gifting, and geography.

Mudrunners are willing to get muddy. They keep going even when adversity strikes. Like Mary, mudrunners realize that Jesus will be with them in any difficulty and that they never run the race alone. No matter the cost, mudrunners do whatever it takes to get the job done and finish the race.

Jesus is looking for more mudrunners with the heart and grit of Mary to advance His kingdom. While you are not Mary, God will use all the wonderful ways He's creatively designed *you* for mud-running. You need only to say with all your heart, "Yes, Jesus, I'm in! I will run the race!"

Your race is before you (perhaps it has already begun!). God has a specific race set for *you* to run. God is waiting for you. And the world is waiting for you. The hurting, dirty, dying, desperate, lost, harassed, helpless, and hopeless are waiting for a Jesus-loving mudrunner who will pull up close, look them in the eye, and offer them Jesus' compassionate message of hope, love, forgiveness, purpose, and life!

If Jesus pulled up a chair to our typical prayer meeting or Bible study, He might hear us requesting prayer for a variety of things: for success in our presentation that week, to do well on a test, for a fun and comfortable day, for a house offer to go through, for our sick cat, or whatever else.

But if we asked Jesus, "What is your prayer request?" I imagine He would immediately and zealously urge us, "Open your eyes and look at the fields! They are ripe for harvest. . . . therefore pray earnestly to the Lord of the harvest to send out laborers into his harvest"! (John 4:35 NIV; Matthew 9:38 ESV).

Amazingly, we can actually become the answer to Jesus' prayer request. It's time for us to start living out His very heartbeat! Will you become the answer to Jesus' prayer request? Will you join the race?

Now What?

- Have you begun the race of advancing God's Kingdom in your everyday life? If yes, In what ways? If no, why not?
- What do you think is unique about the specific race God has for you?
- What specific action step will you take this week to live as a mudrunner?

THREE
THE WHISPER

IN HIGH SCHOOL I was a wrestler and a cross-country runner. Training for wrestling season combined my love for both sports when our coach would send us on a twelve-mile run through a nearby canyon . . . all uphill! It was quite a feat to conquer. I spent months training for just that specific run. But when I think about some of the most significant running events in my life, two other experiences actually come to mind first.

On one such occasion, I was leading a team of high school students on a mission trip to West Africa. Unfortunately, some bad local food was causing urgent stomach issues for me! On our way home, we had a layover in Brussels, Belgium. Our plane landed and we exited. I began to feel the grumbling urges below. I needed a bathroom and quick! So, following the international bathroom symbols along the airport corridor, I scurried to the bathrooms. An older woman with thick glasses and a stoic demeaner stood next to a counter in front of a gate. She was guarding the bathrooms.

The woman declared, "It costs half a euro to use the toilets."

I asked, "Will you take U.S. Dollars? That is all I have."

"No. We only accept local currency, but there is an exchange bank upstairs."

I immediately turned and ran up the stairs. The gurgling rumbles continued!

When I got to the exchange bank, the sign on the door read CLOSED.

I ran back down the stairs to the bathrooms.

I urgently pleaded with the woman: "Please, just let me use your bathrooms. I need to go right away! The exchange bank is closed and I don't have any other money. I will work it out afterward." Time was running out.

She didn't budge. "No. You must pay." (Apparently, she didn't give a crap!)

Panic set in. I mean, it's not like I was alone. I had to lead a team of young people! What could I do to avoid complete disaster?! I ran upstairs to an open coffee shop and shouted, "Does anyone have some money I can borrow? Even a few coins? I need to use the bathroom right away. I don't have any currency to pay, and the exchange bank is closed! Can anyone help me?"

I felt like a fool, but the alternative was much worse. Thankfully someone handed me a few coins.

I ran back downstairs, quickly lunging toward the toilets, handing the woman some money on the way. I barely made it! Let's just say, it's likely that I unintentionally destroyed that toilet.

After flushing and walking back out through the toilet gate, the stern, stiff-spined woman walked over and peered inside. She quickly shot me a horrified glare of disgust. All I could do was shrug, smirk, and keep walking.

No one needed to convince me of the importance of running *to* a toilet in that moment. I knew it.

Another memorable running occasion required me to run *from* something! My friend Nathan and I, along with our ministry partner Mary, had just finished sharing Bible stories with a Hadzabe tribal man in East Africa. We left the man's hut and began the fifteen-minute walk back to our tents. The sun had already gone down. Flashlights in hand, we scanned the landscape as we journeyed. Occasionally, our light reflected back at us as it met with the eyeballs of various animals. Most of what we spotted were dik-diks, which are basically small African deer standing one to two feet tall at best.

As we walked, I thought to myself, *How great would it be if we could hunt down one of these animals and bring it back to the village?! Maybe we could become accepted hunters among them. And we could feast tonight!*

I suggested to Nathan that my fantasy become reality, and the hunt was on! Armed with simple tribal bows, arrows, and a hand-made wooden club, we continued scanning the landscape with our flashlights, searching for more eyeballs reflecting in the night.

Unfortunately, the big hunt soon became unadventurous. Most of the animals ran away from us, zipping left and right as soon as the light exposed them. But then, one didn't run. The animal was hiding in a bush. Unlike the others, the eyeballs on this one appeared much bigger. And it wasn't running, darting, or zipping. As we inched closer, it became clear that whatever it was, it also wasn't budging from the bush.

When we got within a car length of the animal in the bush, an eerie growl hummed from the bush. I turned around to see if Mary might give us insight as to the source of the low-grade rumble. Mary wasn't there. She was dashing the other direction yelling over her shoulder, "Run! It's a lion!"

Mary didn't have to say it twice. Our adrenaline fully engaged, we sprinted in Mary's direction.

"We must run back to camp and start a fire!" Mary instructed.

And run we did! The three of us ran all the way to our tents, quickly sparked a fire, fueled it with brush. On guard and backs to the fire, we peered into the darkness surrounding our camp. Every small noise caught our ears. Every dash of light caused us concern. We prayed that God would protect us. In time, tensions eased, and we were able to rest. The ability to run on that adventurous night proved to be vitally important, so much more than a twelve-mile canyon jaunt to get in shape!

You may not find yourself running *to* a toilet or running *from* a lion, but we all have a race to run, a "race that is set before us" by God Himself (Hebrews 12:1 ESV).

How are *your* running skills? Have you begun the race? Are you holding up? How is your running endurance?

Whatever our pace may be in various seasons and wherever we may find ourselves in the world, running matters. And sometimes this running requires steady perseverance. True perseverance and kingdom grit will keep you running when all you want to do is quit.

I remember one night, while we were engaging the Hadzabe people, when I desperately wanted to quit the race.

I wanted to fold, give in, give up, and go home.

I couldn't sleep. The night was late, but I unzipped the tent and walked into the African bush. During the past week or two we had experienced blow after blow of difficulty and darkness.

Our car had broken down in the middle of nowhere.

New "disciples" had deserted our Bible story meetings for five solid days of drunkenness (I'm talking about passed-out, snotting, can't-stand-up, face-down on-the-ground drunk).

Mary's children had been locked out of their mud-brick home by their deceitful drunk grandmother who left them crying in hunger.

A woman had run into our camp shrieking in fear and pain as blood gushed down her arm, dripping into the dust. She had been attacked by a man who demanded that she cook a meal for him. She cooked it, but he didn't like the food. So he assaulted her.

We witnessed a young Hadzabe girl die.

Like I said, it was a very difficult week. The horizon appeared dark and gloomy, and I wanted to quit.

As I walked through the darkness of night, I prayed out loud as I fumed with anger and frustration: "Lord, none of this seems to be working! Are we wasting our time? We are investing all our time equipping these few tribals who said yes to you, Jesus. But now they have been drunk for five days straight! And what about the girl who died in front of our eyes! I still don't understand. Why would you let that happen? Are we having any impact here at all? Should we just give up now, pack our bags, and go home?"

As I wandered around the bush outside our camp, everything felt hopeless. All the obstacles seemed insurmountable. It felt like we had been running through a jungle only to hit quicksand—and now we were up to our necks in muddy impossibilities.

And yet . . .

Why were we so surprised?

Running the race and treading mud go hand in hand. It's not the exception, it's the norm. It's to be expected!

Count on it: as we run this race, we *will* hit mud! If you haven't already, be assured, the mud will come. You may slip and slide. You'll most likely sink in a little further than you expect. At times, the mud will grab hold of you and try to hold you back. You may even wonder for a moment, *Will I make it out?* You may be running the best you know how and still be stuck with muddy thoughts like *Where am I going? Am I useless? Can God really use me? Is there any purpose in running this race?*

Maybe that's why we are urged to "run *with endurance* the race that is set before us" (Hebrews 12:1 ESV, italics mine). As we run, perseverance will be necessary. The trail will get wet, slippery, slimy, and slick. And yes, at times, altogether muddy.

How can we keep going in the midst of the mud? How can we become those who run through it? Even more, how can we become those who *embrace* the challenge of mud? How can we move beyond living as mud avoiders to become true mudrunners?

As I wandered alone in the dark that night feeling helpless, hopeless, and stuck in thick mud, I looked up into the sky and took note of something that changed everything.

I saw several bright stars that formed the shape of a house. Along with the God-inspired image in the stars, these words echoed in my heart: *"Charlie, don't worry. I will build my house among the Hadzabe people."*

Although they came as a still small voice, these words were fresh, stable, strong, and full of peace as they entered my mind.

They certainly were not my words. I knew without a doubt that they were from the Lord!

Through this message in the stars, Jesus was giving me a keep-going whisper! *"Keep going, Charlie! I've got this. I will make it happen."*

I was immediately filled with peace, trusting that God would have His way. I was able to keep going. I was even able to embrace the difficulty, darkness, and impossibility that seemed to glare back in my face. It didn't matter anymore. Jesus was bigger than all of it, and I was running the race that He had specifically set in front of me.

Hebrews 12 gives us insight on embracing the mud. We are encouraged to become mudrunners by looking to Jesus and considering Jesus, who endured the mud! In this way we will "not grow weary or fainthearted" (Hebrews 12:2–3 ESV). This is the key to kingdom grit.

Jesus is the one who will carry you through. He is there with you in the race and He won't leave your side! In the muddy valley of death, don't lose sight of Him. Take your eyes off the impossibility and fix them on the One who endured and overcame. Seek His life-giving whisper. To become a mudrunner, you must look to *the* original Mudrunner, Jesus Himself!

May you reach the end of your race and hear Jesus say—muddy as you may be—"Well done, good and faithful runner! You ran well the race I laid out for you."

In the meantime, endure. Listen for Jesus' "keep going" whisper. Mud *will* come, but so will the finish line. So, look to Jesus. Did you catch that? Look to Jesus. Got it? Are you sure? Look to Jesus!

Now What?

- In the midst of mud, these negative thoughts began to plague my mind: *Where am I going? Am I useless? Can God really use me? Is there any purpose in running this race?* In what ways do doubts or inadequacies tend to creep up on you and hinder you from God's purpose in your life?

- When have you wanted to quit and give up on God and life? What helped you to move forward?
- Starting this week, how will you begin looking to Jesus in all you do?

FOUR

RADICAL AUTHORITY

NATHAN QUICKLY SCARFED down his lunch, walked out of the farmhouse, and picked up a shovel. He made his way over to a ditch where one of the locals was digging. Without a word, Nathan joined the worker in deepening the trench.

Peering into the field, I wondered what Nathan was doing. Not only was he digging, Nathan appeared to be talking—a strange event given I knew he didn't speak the local language. What could he possibly be saying? Nathan was certainly piquing my curiosity. I enjoyed the wonder along with my soup and headed out to complete the workday.

Later that afternoon, I asked Nathan, "What were you doing out there with that worker earlier?"

"I felt like God wanted me to serve that man by digging with him," Nathan answered. "And as I did, God prompted me to pray out loud the entire time. I prayed for his country, for the man, his family, and that each of them would come to know Jesus." Nathan paused, then added, "I just continued to pray while we dug."

As Nathan and I continued to talk, one of the nonlocal, English-speaking farm workers walked over to join us.

"Nathan," he said, "I noticed you were digging a trench with Mr. Park. Did you have any good conversations with him?"

"What do you mean?" Nathan answered with a bit of a puzzled head tilt.

"He is one of the few locals here who knows English."

"Wow! Are you serious?" replied Nathan. "That's crazy! The truth is we never had a conversation because I just assumed he didn't know English! I was simply obeying what the Lord had prompted me to do."

Nathan's encounter with the worker that day was significant. While the conversation was God-led and equally heartwarming, Nathan's out-loud and unknowingly understood prayers invited great risk. Nathan and I had been volunteering alongside local residents in arguably the most dangerous and restricted country for Christians. This is no easy place to share the gospel, and those who are caught doing so face extreme consequences. Therefore, kingdom opportunity in this place is incredibly rare, yet still, Jesus orchestrated an unbelievable open door for Nathan to walk through.

When we first began to consider traveling to this country, I did not think it would be possible. I wasn't sure their restrictive Communist regime would allow someone from a free country to enter, let alone someone who is a Christian. However, the more I read about what was happening there—the extremely violent human rights violations as well as the politically induced fear and shame—and how little access people had to the gospel, the more I felt drawn to go. As I prayed for the country, I felt God tugging on my heart and prompting me to pursue the trip.

In time I discovered going *was* possible! Still, even with such great news, I began assessing the risk. My head was swirling with all kinds of cautions: *Should we really go to this place? Isn't it a bit risky? Who are we to be the ones going to a place like that?* I knew any risk for the gospel was worth taking, yet saying out loud, "We are taking a trip to the one of the most dangerous and restricted countries in the world," came with a certain measure of uneasiness.

This country was saying to the world, "Do not bring the gospel to us!"

People I respected were saying to me, "Charlie, don't go. It is too risky. It doesn't seem wise to go."

But I knew I must seek out God's will above all else. He is in fact the one with all authority, which means He is in charge of it all (Matthew 28:18). He must be the one we obey before all others.

So I prayed. *God, I want to be sure You are calling us to go to this country. I don't want to just jump out on an adventurous whim. Lord, just as Gideon sought You to confidently know that what he was about to embark on was Your idea and not his own (Judges 6), would You give me a sign it is really You talking to me?*

At the time I was single. My wife and I had met but were simply friends at that point. I had shared a little with her about the country and how I was considering going there. I never asked her to pray about it. I never asked for a response. I just shared what I was pondering. Little did I know at the time that God would use her as the answer to my prayer.

I had prayed for a sign. The very next day, God used my future wife to bring the trip confirmation I needed.

"I don't usually do this," she said, "but I need to tell you something."

"What is it? Be free."

"I had a dream last night. I saw a woman speaking, and she said, 'Charlie and Nathan have a burden for that country for a reason.' I'm not sure if that means anything to you, but I felt like God wanted me to share it."

"That is amazing! I can hardly believe this!" I declared. "I was praying just yesterday that God would give me a sign that it is really Him talking to me, and that He would confirm whether or not we are really supposed to take this trip. This is it. I guess we are going!" The one with all authority had spoken.

Little did I know, by the time Nathan and I would be on the ground in that country, I would be engaged to my wife. God knew that my fiancé would also need a strong word from Him about this trip. She would need to be on board with it to send me off in peace, fully knowing the risks involved. In God's sovereignty, He did just that. I was beginning to see glimpses of His power and authority at work among us! He really was in charge of it all, and He still is.

Authority naturally demands submission. We would only take intense risks to obey someone with incredible authority! But authority also connotes the one who oversees something. And only *the One* with *all* authority, overseeing the entire universe, could bring together all the pieces of the puzzle in such a powerful way.

The Scriptures declare that after Jesus rose from the dead, He was seated at the right hand of the throne of God far above all rule, above all authority, above all power, above all dominion, and given the name that is above every other name (Ephesians 1:20–21)! Jesus holds all authority! His authority over heaven, earth, and everything in between really shines through in both urgent, weighty situations as well as small moments along the way. Jesus is in charge of the big vision and the small details of our lives. Nothing exists outside His purview. There is nothing too big for Jesus. There are no obstacles nor hindrances we cannot overcome with the one who holds all authority. We just have to keep our spiritual eyes open to see this reality.

I remember a time when Nathan and I were waiting for a flight with multiple upcoming complicated connections. As I watched the screen above the attendants, the delay continued to grow. It would not be good if this delay caused us to miss our next leg of flights. International flight delays and changes are quite an ordeal! We finally boarded the plane and hoped for the best.

As soon as the wheels touched down on the tarmac, I turned my phone on and anxiously waited for a cell connection. *Ding!* The message hit my screen: "Your connecting flight has already departed." My heart sank.

The news was disheartening, but something inside me said, "Just run to your next gate and see what happens." Nathan and I sprinted through the airport for nearly a mile. As our hearts pounded and minds raced wondering what might happen, we spotted the sign for our flight. It felt like a miraculous sighting: our plane was still there!

Huffing, puffing, and with barely the breath to speak, we approached the gate and held out our tickets. The gate attendant, as if she knew our whole ordeal, said joyfully, "Welcome aboard, you made it! You're the last two to board the flight."

A message of discouragement. A prompting to run. A mission saved. Coincidence? I don't think so. Did God hold that plane just for us? Maybe. I wouldn't put it past Him. Here's what I know without a doubt: Jesus has all authority, and as the God who rules the universe, He is certainly able to hold any plane, anytime, for anyone, for His kingdom purposes!

God's authority really does make a difference—in small things (simply hoping we make our plane) and big things (opening doors to see the gospel proclaimed in the most difficult places around the globe), and everything in between. He has authority over every walkable inch of the globe—and on every unwalkable inch too. He has authority in the tangible and intangible, in the physical and in the spiritual realm. Jesus is in charge of everything. He has all authority. And it makes all the difference.

When Jesus first called His disciples, He called them to His mission, to become "fishers of men" (Mark 1:17 ESV). Just after He called them, the very first thing Jesus exemplified for them was His authority (see Mark 1:17–28). And just before He ascended, the very last thing Jesus said to His disciples was "All authority in heaven and on earth has been given to me. Therefore go and make disciples of all nations" (Matthew 28:18–19 NIV).

Jesus linked His mission with His authority in the beginning and in the end. Therefore, His authority must make all the difference in the big, the small, and in everything in between, not only for them but for us too.

As we step into God's unique purpose for our lives and step out for His global kingdom cause, opposition will arise. Darkness will oppose His purposes. People will resist His plans. Yet no matter what comes against, we must obey God rather than men (Acts 5:29). He is the one we are accountable to. He has all authority in heaven and on Earth. Therefore, we must look first to our King who holds all authority in our lives. But we can be assured that no person, no plan, and no power can stop Jesus! And this Jesus is the one overseeing every detail of our lives.

Venturing into a restricted country, Nathan's urge to dig and pray for the local who "happened to know English," my wife's mysterious dream, a quiet prompting to run to a "missed flight": all of these declare that Jesus, the one with all authority, is truly in charge of it all, no matter the circumstance!

I would even venture to call His authority a radical authority.

Have you been living with a confident perspective based on the radical authority of Jesus? What difference could His authority make in your life?

Now What?

- How have you understood, or how would you have described, the authority of Jesus up to this point in your life?
- Do you find yourself more often living for the approval and demands of others (who attempt to exert their own "authority" over you) or simply living for the approval of God?
- What difference does it make in your life to understand that Jesus has all authority? Maybe there's a situation in your life that looks impossible or daunting. What if you asked the one with all authority how He views this situation; what might He show you?

FIVE

COMPELLED BY . . . ?

"WAIT! STOP THE CAR!" I exclaimed. "Before heading down the other side of these mountains, we should stop in this village."

Sitting in the Land Cruiser, we debated: share the message of Jesus with this village on the way or move swiftly to the village at the bottom of the other side?

"I just don't have peace about staying here," Nathan asserted.

I counterpointed with a compromise. "What if we do this: spend one day in this village to share the gospel and the next day be on our way?"

Up to this point, we had been staying in a small village lodged between this mountain range and a sizable salt lake. God had burdened our hearts with a village just on the other side of the mountain ridge. So we had begun the journey. As we drove through bushes, trees, and over rocks, we had reached our current location on the top of the mountain. The nearby village was mysteriously located behind rocks, vines, and all sorts of trees and bushes that were intertwined together. It was amazing that a car could even get through this place.

As we came to a halt, I hopped out of the Land Cruiser. "I'll be back in a few minutes. We need to pray," I told Nathan, Mary, and Emmanuel.

We needed the Lord's direction. I thought walking and praying might help. However, I decided not to wander too far lest I become the answer to the dinner prayer of a lion, elephant, pack of hyenas, or some other wild beast. Slowly, I walked around while intently praying, "Lord, do You want us to go directly to the next village or spend more time here?"

I listened for God's response. Moments later, these words flooded my mind: *It humanly makes sense to stay and share. But I want you to pass the village and go on.* It seemed the Spirit of God was leading us to something far beyond my vision or ideas.

I returned to the car. "I was wrong, Nathan," I confessed. "Having prayed, I believe God wants us to keep going. So let's keep moving." We continued our adventure through the bush.

The rugged terrain made for a long journey, but by the day's end we arrived in the village on the other side of the ridge. As we rolled in, Mary pitched in to give direction. "We need to gain the village leader's permission to stay in the area and share with the people."

"Okay, let's go find him," I agreed.

We walked to the village leader's hut. While I had no idea what would happen next, it became a kingdom moment I will never forget.

Village chiefs hold all the cards for their villages—who comes, who goes, what happens, what doesn't. They are the ones in charge. In other words, the village chief holds all authority for the village. This village chief was no different. And what was his verdict to our petition? He demanded, "To stay you must pay!"

Here's the problem we had with his ultimatum. We knew the money we'd pay would go directly to life-taking, not life-giving, things. We were well aware of what they often used such payouts for: binge drinking homemade liquor from other tribes, getting high as a kite off local *bangi*, otherwise known to them as "mir-ah-jah-wawn-ah" (yes, it is what it sounds like).

The dilemma began. Should we pay them or somehow withhold the money? Was the cost worth it? Nathan, Emmanuel, Mary, and I discussed possible solutions and came up with a plan we believed would satisfy the village chief.

"We will give each family who comes to our camp a bucket of corn flour for food as well as an audio Bible," we offered. "You have never had the Bible in your language, and there are freshly translated Bible stories on these players. We would like to give these as gifts to each family if you allow us to stay."

The village chief stood silent. He cocked his head slightly left then right as if he were adding numbers in his head. His decision made, he answered Mary in his native tongue.

Mary delivered his verdict to the rest of us: "He will not agree."

It felt like we were in an impossible situation. What on earth could we do? This was clearly the village the Spirit of God had led us to. But the door seemed closed. More accurately, it felt boarded up and bolted shut.

"What are we going to do?" I asked our team. "Mary, you have the most experience with these situations. Do you have any ideas?"

Little did I know, a book-of-Acts moment was about to unfold before our very eyes. Mary—a soft-spoken, petite, introverted woman who is equally gentle, humble, and kind—raised her head, looked firmly at the village chief, and addressed him with conviction in her voice.

"That's fine," Mary said to the man who possessed less authority than he knew. "We won't pay you. We will just leave. But I want you to know something . . ."

Mary held not only the chief's attention but now his curiosity. "You won't only be chasing us away," she continued, "but you will be chasing away the Holy Spirit who lives inside of us. And you surely do *not* want to do that!"

Mary's response floored me. *Mary,* I thought, *are you kidding me? I've never seen you so ferocious! Where did all that boldness come from? Did you seriously just say something like that to a chief? Do we need to quickly get outta here?*

With my head still swirling from the events of the moment,

the chief responded. His tone and demeanor reversed course. "Okay, no problem," he offered. "You guys can stay and do whatever you want."

Later that evening, I asked Mary, "Where did you come up with that response? Where did those words come from?"

"I felt the Holy Spirit rising up within me. It's like the words bubbled up inside me, and God's power gave me the ability to speak them to the village leader."

The Holy Spirit led Mary outside the four walls of her home and far beyond her comfort zone. Surely He had something up His sleeve!

God had made a way to get into this village after all. One by one, provisions began falling into place. A man kindly allowed us to stay near his hut. We set up our tents, found three rocks to build a cooking fire, and began making dinner for the night.

The next morning a crowd began to form around our camp. The word had already spread that we had free food and audio Bibles. People came from all over to meet us and receive food to fill their stomachs. What they didn't know is that many of them would also find the satisfaction they longed for spiritually.

As many tribals gathered around us, we began to preach the gospel. We knew this tribe worshiped the sun as their traditional god. So, we told them the story of Jesus from creation to the cross —how He rose from the dead and that anyone who follows Jesus can have a relationship with the living God, both now and for eternity.

"This God we proclaim to you created the sun," we told them. "God is higher than the sun. If you want to believe in Jesus, you must no longer worship the sun but only worship Jesus."

We concluded the message with an invitation to the gathered crowd. "Who wants to stop worshiping *Ishoko* [the name of their sun god] and start following Jesus?" we asked. The invitation echoed Jesus' offer to His first disciples when He said, "Come follow me."

Someone in the crowd spoke up. "We all want to follow Jesus!"

"This is not something you can decide for everyone," we told the well-meaning man. "Those of you who are truly serious about giving your life to Jesus, come forward in front of everyone here."

People began to shuffle. By our count, eleven Hadzabe people stepped forward. They were serious in their surrender to Jesus. We all prayed together as they began a newfound friendship with Jesus —through whom and for whom all things were made, including the sun (Colossians 1:16).

We ended our prayer by singing, "I Have Decided to Follow Jesus," which had recently been translated into Hadzabe click language. As we sang these truths together, there was an elderly woman at the edge of the crowd leaning against the trunk of a baobab tree. Tears began flowing down her cheeks. It seemed this woman was experiencing peace unlike she had ever experienced— the peace of Jesus surpassing anything we can logically understand. Jesus gripped her life and changed her heart in an instant. This one moment would affect eternity.

Two of the young men who gave their lives to Jesus began to spend more time with us that evening. That was exactly what we hoped for. While Jesus preached to crowds, He also multiplied followers through up-close time with a few. We desired to do the same. The spiritual hunger of these young men astonished me. It was so much greater than any spiritual hunger I had yet encountered among the Hadzabe tribe. We shared time around the fire that evening teaching them more and more about life with Jesus.

Before our evening ended and we headed for our tents, one of these young men shared his gratitude. "I wish I had more time with you," he said, "but I must leave now, because tomorrow morning I am traveling to another region to work on a farm."

Almighty God knew all the details. God knew that this young Hadza man desperately needed Him. God knew the man was spiritually hungry and searching for more. God knew the urgency we needed to have in getting to this village for the sake of one man's life. If we would have stopped at the other village along the way, we would have missed this man's life completely. It is likely that he would not have heard the gospel, he would not have believed, and we would not have been able to share with him. But God knew. In

His sovereignty God increased our urgency to get to this specific village for this one specific life. And His kingdom movement came among us!

How did all of this happen in the village that day? What sparked it? I am convinced all of it was made possible because one woman was compelled by something greater than comfort and security. Mary stepped out of her cultural bounds and stepped up to a village chief, risking her reputation, safety, and so much more.

What would compel her to do such a thing? Only the kingdom of God. Mary was compelled by God and His kingdom more than her comfort. She believed in the urgency of bringing the message of Jesus to the lost and seeing Jesus made King among them. So much so, Mary chose to forsake her comfort for this cause. And in her determination to choose God's kingdom over her comfort, Mary became the spiritual tipping point for an entire village.

In Luke 9, Jesus pulls up close to three guys to have a conversation about their comfort zones. Jesus shared the hard truth that the kingdom must be a greater priority than their home, their culture, and even their closest friends and family (Luke 9:57–62). These guys all had similar responses: "Lord, first let me . . ." Each of these guys had a *first* other than Jesus and His kingdom. Something else or someone else took a higher priority in their lives. They found their security in other places and were stuck living lives of comfort.

We don't know how they responded to Jesus at the end of the day. The story doesn't say. But we do know how *we* can respond to Jesus. Jesus reveals that if we want to live a life of impact, His kingdom must have first priority in our life (Matthew 6:33). Jesus seems to say, "If you really want to run the race, it starts with making Me your number one priority." Jesus led anyone who followed Him to step outside their comfort zone, and His Spirit is still leading us to do the same today! The only question is, Will we embrace His invitation to boldly step outside the four walls of our home, our church, and our friend groups?

Now What?

- Do you have "comfort zones" that have taken first priority in your life, more than Jesus and His kingdom cause for the world? Talk with Him about laying them down.
- What would it look like for you to join Mary and others who are compelled by God's kingdom more than their comfort zones?
- Read Luke 10:1, 9, 17–21 to see what happened to those who embraced Jesus' invitation. What might happen if you stepped out to embrace Jesus' invitation in your life?

SIX

THE WATCHMAN

ON A VERY BUSINESS-AS-USUAL day while back in the States, my phone buzzed. Pulling the phone from my pocket, I noticed it was a text from Mary, our key Hadzabe partner. The three-word message was short and to the point: MAMOYA HAS PASSED.

This was heavy news. Our friend Mamoya was leaving behind his wife and several children who needed provision and care. Barely four months before Mamoya's passing, one of their children suddenly died. The family was just getting back on their feet. I couldn't help but think how this tragedy would surely knock them back on their knees.

Mamoya was an honorable man and good father. And even more, he had an insatiable hunger for Jesus and His Word. I began recalling all the time we spent together as he asked question after question about what it meant to follow Jesus. Mamoya's heart burned with Christlike passion and reflected Jesus' love.

While we had lost a dear friend, family member, and faithful kingdom-laboring servant here on earth, I was confident Mamoya was face-to-face with Jesus. Even in grief, is there any greater hope or joy than that?

Death has a way of always recentering my focus on eternity. It did that day, and it would again; this would not be the last death notice I would receive.

It was a few years later that Mary sent another report of tough news. As with her message about Mamoya, Mary's text was brief: ONWAS HAS DIED. Accompanying Mary's texts were pictures of the Hadzabe burying his body. News like that doesn't always seem real when received halfway around the world. Yet the photos Mary included were sobering.

The news of Onwas's death immediately saddened me. Yet as with the news of Mamoya, I rejoiced that Onwas had received the gospel several years back and was now face-to-face with the living God. Onwas had always been like our Hadzabe "grandfather." He was also a famous tribal elder among the people and had strong influence over many.

When I met Onwas, he did not know the gospel nor what Jesus had done for him. I had the opportunity to witness Onwas receive the gospel and grow in hunger for God's Word. I wondered how many of the Hadzabe people had been open to Jesus because of Onwas's wide influence.

Hearing of his passing, I recalled the day Onwas first heard the Scriptures in his own language. With a smile on his face he immediately repeated all the words back to us. Emphatically and joyfully, Onwas assured us he could finally comprehend every single word of Scripture! I remembered how the gospel caused this elderly man to dance and sing for Jesus, tribal-bush style—walking in place, swinging his arms back and forth, and shaking his head side to side to the rhythm of the beat in his heart. These vivid memories caused my heart to leap with joy for this man who was now in heaven. And yet his loss was heavy to me and many others who loved him.

I texted Mary back: I AM SO SORRY TO HEAR ABOUT ONWAS. HOW ARE YOU DOING, AND HOW ARE THE PEOPLE DOING WITH HIS DEATH?

Mary quickly replied: ALL OF HIS FAMILY AND ALL THE

Hadzabe who were there were very sad to lose someone, especially an elder in God's mission.

In hopeful agreement, I sent another message: We are sad, but we are also rejoicing. Now, Onwas is dancing before the throne of God and worshipping Jesus for all eternity!

Yes, Mary affirmed, we hope to meet each other and sing together in heaven!

My last memory of Onwas included, of all things, oatmeal. I had given him a new audio Bible and some packets of oatmeal on our last venture. He loved oatmeal! He couldn't get enough of it! Whenever we camped near his village, he would come over in the morning, sit down, and wait for us to share our oatmeal. I was often amazed at how many oatmeal packets Onwas would empty into his cup: three, sometimes even four, at a time! We began to understand that the way to Onwas's heart was through a warm bowl of oatmeal! That's why we made a point to stop and give Onwas that treasured gift every time we passed by his village.

Most Hadzabe people claim baboon brains as their favorite food. Not Onwas. His favorite was clearly oatmeal. While Jesus was clearly first in his life, oatmeal was high on his list. And when I think of how much Onwas loved Jesus—and enjoyed oatmeal—I'm reminded of the Scripture that says, "Taste and see that the Lord is good" (Psalm 34:8 niv).

Take a moment to remember some of the best moments you've ever had with Jesus. If you've ever experienced His goodness, I bet it left you longing for more—just like the first bite of your favorite meal. One taste isn't really enough to fill your craving, is it?

Now imagine combining all of your greatest moments with Jesus into one massively extraordinary experience. The Bible declares that whatever we experience of God right now is only a foretaste of what is to come when we see Jesus face-to-face! All of our best moments with Him on Earth pale in comparison to our eternal worship and enjoyment of His presence.

We are also promised to experience the joy of being reunited with our Christian brothers and sisters who have died. We will receive pain-free resurrected bodies, all suffering will be done away with, all war and division will cease, every tear will be wiped away, and all that is broken will be restored. I long for the day when Jesus will return. *Come, Lord Jesus!* is often my heart's prayer. How about you? Do you long for Jesus' return? It's hard for me to imagine anyone who wouldn't long for freedom, joy, and the absence of heartache and pain.

That said, are we willing to do what Jesus has said must be done before He returns? When Jesus' disciples asked when the end of the world would come, Jesus answered, "This gospel of the kingdom will be preached in the whole world as a testimony to all nations, and then the end will come" (Matthew 24:14 NIV).

The gospel will be proclaimed among all nations (i.e., ethno-linguistic people groups, or tribes) and *then* the end will come. Before Jesus ascended back to heaven, He gave us our marching orders and sent us out to complete the mission: proclaim the good news among all the unreached of the world. If we want Jesus to return, we must go! We must share . . . with our neighbors, with our city, with our country, with the world! As far as we are able, we must go. As much as it is possible, we must share. To the greatest degree we can sacrifice, we must help mobilize others for His mission. Jesus' final command must be our first concern!

The words of Ezekiel have continued to remind me of eternal realities and grip me with conviction:

> *The word of the Lord came to me: "Son of man, speak to your people and say to them: 'When I bring the sword against a land, and the people of the land choose one of their men and make him their watchman, and he sees the sword coming against the land and blows the trumpet to warn the people, then if anyone hears the trumpet but does not heed the warning and the sword comes and takes their life, their blood will be on their own head. Since they heard the sound of the trumpet but did not heed the warning, their blood will be*

on their own head. If they had heeded the
warning, they would have saved themselves. But
if the watchman sees the sword coming and does
not blow the trumpet to warn the people and the
sword comes and takes someone's life, that person's
life will be taken because of their sin, but I will
hold the watchman accountable for their blood'"
(Ezekiel 33:2–6 NIV).

God tells Ezekiel that he is a spiritual watchman for Israel, charged with the responsibility of warning others about the coming judgment for their sin. If Ezekiel warns the people and they perish, the people themselves will be responsible for their deaths and he will be free. But if Ezekiel fails to warn them, he will be held responsible for their deaths (Ezekiel 33:7-9).

Now, why would these seemingly obscure words about a prophet's calling in the Old Testament grip me? Well, if it were not for Paul the apostle, these words would be less weighty than I believe they are. When the Jews opposed and reviled Paul for proclaiming the gospel, he alluded to Ezekiel's warning in addressing them: "Your blood be on your own heads! I am innocent. From now on I will go to the Gentiles!" (Acts 18:6 ESV). And again Paul says among Gentiles, "I testify to you this day that I am innocent of the blood of all, for I did not shrink from declaring to you the whole counsel of God" (Acts 20:26–27 ESV), or as another translation states, "I declare today that I have been faithful. If anyone suffers eternal death, it's not my fault for I didn't shrink from declaring all that God wants you to know" (Acts 20:26–27 NLT). Essentially, Paul is saying, "I have proclaimed the gospel to you, but the response is up to you. Therefore, I am clear of my responsibility. Your eternal consequences are on your own head now!"

It is clear. We must proclaim the gospel. It is our responsibility as believers! In fact, we have even been called Christ's ambassadors. God has always orchestrated His kingdom movement through His people. The Bible does not mince words: without someone preaching to them, people may never hear and therefore never believe and never receive salvation (Romans 10:14).

God has chosen to work through us. But what happens if we don't proclaim? What happens when we see all the lost and hopeless people around us clearly on their way to eternal destruction and do nothing? We often ask, "What happens to those who never hear about Jesus?" But I think a better question is, "What happens to those of us who know but never go, those of us who never proclaim the good news of Jesus?"

The passing of my Hadzabe friends Mamoya and Onwas got me thinking. I couldn't help but consider all of these Scriptures. What if we had never gone? What if we had never shared the good news with them? What if we had disobeyed God's call? Would they have been missed completely? Would they be spending eternity without Christ? Or would God have raised up others to go?

I like to think the latter is true, but I cannot live with the certainty that it is guaranteed. If we had not gone, we might have had Onwas's blood on our heads. We might have been held responsible for his spiritual life. Now, what would that look like exactly? I have no idea. But I can tell you whatever it is, I do not want to experience the weight of it!

What I do know with absolute certainty is that we would have missed out on the joy of joining Jesus in His mission, and we would have never known the joy of Onwas's life and friendship.

Simply put, I'm really glad we went. I am filled with such reassurance and gladness that we did not give up when things got hard nor did we allow difficulties to detour us from God's desires. Onwas's life (and death) compel me to share the gospel with even more people. They've solidified my resolve never to miss a single opportunity God has for me to share Him with others!

Life is too short to stay cocooned within our comfort zones. And, if I am honest, I am tempted to spend my life there more often than I want to admit. But I have watched too many people die and have felt the weight of eternity too often to waste the kingdom opportunities God brings. I don't know about you, but like Ezekiel, I long to be the best watchman I can possibly be!

Death has a way of getting us to think about the reality of eternity—what is at stake and what really matters in this life.

It just so happens that on the day I received the news of Onwas's death, I was preaching at a camp for youth and young adults. I had not planned on giving an invitation for missions at the end of my message, but I felt the Holy Spirit compelling me so strongly that I couldn't do anything else! I invited the crowd to consider whether God was calling them to the mission field. Amazingly, seventeen people immediately jumped to their feet, saying, "God is calling me to go to the nations!"

Although I felt deep sadness at Onwas's passing, it was actually a glorious day. Onwas ran his race and reached the finish line *and* seventeen young runners began their races to potentially some of the muddiest places around the globe. Death was overshadowed by new life that day. For those who trust and obey Christ, light and life always conquer darkness and death.

God is raising up an army of those who will enlist and live as faithful watchmen (and yes, watchwomen!). Will you join them in the race? Will you fulfill the charge? Having read this chapter, you know too much to do nothing!

Now What?

- Why do you think Paul alluded to Ezekiel's picture of a watchman to describe our role in God's mission?
- Have you ever considered the responsibility we have as believers to proclaim the message of Jesus to the whole world? How do you process this reality?
- What can you do to fulfill your role as God's watchman or watchwoman?

SEVEN

THE SIMPLICITY OF THE MESSAGE

AS WE FULFILL the charge as watchmen, what is the message we're called to proclaim?

After dinner we sat around a well-used wooden table and drank tea. Beyond the seasoned windows of this local guesthouse, picturesque views of the Himalayas declared the glory of God. My Asian friends and I sipped on our hot drinks and discussed the joys, victories, and difficulties of God's mission.

Aliza shared amazing testimonies of God's glory breaking through. "I pray for many people in the name of Jesus and they are often healed!" she said. "I think God has given me this spiritual gift. I also have been sharing the gospel with many of them."

"How have people been responding to the gospel message?" I inquired.

Aliza continued. "Some are interested, but right now my family is the only Christian family in our village. Harsh opposition and persecution pose daily difficulties for us. In earlier days, villagers threw rocks and placed curses on our home. Their actions did not have the outcome they hoped for. The people of the village were amazed that their curses had no power over us or our home.

Jesus has protected us. Even still, most in the village are resistant to the message of Jesus."

"How do the people show their resistance? What do they do?" I was curious to learn more.

Aliza was glad to give more insight. "There is a village just up from mine. The people of this village will beat you with sticks if you try to talk about Jesus. Now that I've shared about Jesus a few times there, they're on the lookout for me. They know what I'm there to do. The last time I went, people threw rocks at me, and I had to run away to safety."

"You have amazing courage, Aliza!" I exclaimed, feeling blessed just to sit with a sister of such courageous faith.

I felt led to share a story from a neighboring region that involved someone Aliza knew, a man named Purna. "You know, Aliza, I trekked into a nearby village with Purna one time. Although he claims to be a true Christian, he was a strong barrier to the gospel. As we were walking through the village, we saw an older woman who was sobbing. She told us about some family problems she was struggling with. So, we began to encourage her, sharing about the love and reassuring presence of Jesus. God was gripping her heart and meeting the woman in her need. At one point, she said, 'I want to follow Jesus, but there is no one here to teach me.' She was ready to believe in Jesus right there!

"But Purna said, 'She cannot believe in Jesus now because she is worried about who will bury her body when she dies. She says that the Buddhists will not bury her if she follows Jesus, and there are no Christians in her village to bury her when she dies. So, she cannot believe until there is a full-time pastor there.' I was furious! Purna did not want to talk about the reality of resurrection—how she didn't need to worry about her body but rather her eternity. Nor did Purna think to offer himself as a solution to her burial quandary. Personally, I was willing to offer to fly from the U.S. and make the long trek to her village for the sole purpose of having her funeral and burying her if that's what was necessary for her to say yes to Jesus. But Purna did not want to discuss it. He literally shut the kingdom of heaven in this woman's face as we walked away."

Aliza replied, "Yes, I do know that man, Purna. I have seen a shift in his attitude. For some reason, something has changed him."

Aadesh piped in, "You know, he will have to give an account one day for that. He will be held responsible."

"Yes, that is true," I said. "I surely would not want to have that on my head." My thoughts turned once again to the watchman passages in Ezekiel.

As our conversation spilled late into the evening, Aadesh took a turn. He shared about the training we had done for the village believers that day. "The training was very effective," he asserted. "I liked how it equipped everyone to share the gospel in a simple way along with their own story of how Jesus has changed them."

Aadesh later shared some deeper, more personal thoughts. "You know, I had one friend who I always wanted to share the gospel with," he said. "I kept thinking, *I will share with him sometime!* But I kept putting it off. Recently, he died. To this day I regret never having shared the gospel with my friend. This training, however, has given me confidence for how I can share with other friends in the future."

Kalit had been listening intently as everyone told their stories about our day together. Now it was his turn to share. "Yes, the training was very helpful for all the believers in this village! Everyone here always knew they needed to share the gospel and make disciples, but they were not always sure *how* to share nor *what* to share. After today, they have realized that the message can be shared anywhere with anyone, even in a short time. It does not have to be done in a building or take extreme amounts of time. It can be done simply."

When I finally laid down in my bed that night, I couldn't sleep. My heart was full and my head, busy. I kept replaying the many powerful stories and raw testimonies that our faithful brothers and sister in Christ had shared.

Equally, my heart was heavy. I was burdened for Sabita, who was the owner, cook, and hostess at the guesthouse where we were staying. We happened to be the only guests lodging there for these few days. I knew she was a Buddhist, and I felt compelled to share Jesus with her.

Our village friends are not the only ones who often feel the pressure of *what* to share or *how* to share it. I have often felt this way; I imagine you have too. That night, I laid awake praying and thinking about how I might share the good news with Sabita. We were leaving the next morning, so I would only have one shot at it. I thought, *Let's put this training into action!*

We awoke early the next morning to prepare for our long journey. I quickly consumed my bread and tea breakfast so that I could share with our friend Sabita. The last several days I had worked hard to love her intentionally and actively by learning her name, asking her questions, and complimenting her hard work at the guesthouse. Now was the time to love her with my words.

"Sabita, I wanted to share a few words with you before we leave. You are doing an incredible job here. Thank you for your hard work and delicious food!"

"Thank you, and you are welcome!" she replied with a smile.

"In my life I used to believe that a good job, a good amount of money, and a good family would satisfy me. The harder I worked for these things to bring me satisfaction and meaning in life, the less they actually did. Then one day I was praying, and Jesus began speaking to me. I began spending more time with Jesus, and He satisfied me more than anything I could ever imagine."

As Sabita listened, I continued, "In Buddhism, you do many good things so that you will receive blessings and spiritual protection. But in Christianity Jesus lived a perfectly holy life and died for all the bad things we have done. Then He rose from the dead, so He is alive today. That is why we can have a true relationship with the one true God. I do not know what you think about this, but I wanted to tell you before we left."

Sabita replied, "I do like this idea. I might do this one day."

I encouraged her, "Do not wait too long. Life is short, and you do not want to miss out on all that Jesus has for you."

"Thank you," Sabita said as she smiled. "Please stay in our guesthouse if you come again!"

"We surely will!" I replied. "Thanks again!" I walked away full of joy, assured I had done what God asked. I rejoiced that God had given me the words I needed for the special opportunity and brief amount of time I was given.

In just a few minutes, Sabita became intrigued by a simple message. Aadesh, Kalit, and others had also discovered the power of a simple message in their own evangelistic efforts.

Sometimes we make the good news inaccessible by making it too complicated—not only to the lost but also to ourselves. I often wonder if Satan likes it that way. After all, Paul wrote to the Corinthians, "I am afraid that, as the serpent deceived Eve by his craftiness, your minds will be led astray from the *simplicity* and purity of devotion to Christ" (2 Corinthians 11:3 NASB, italics mine).

I am amazed by the simplicity of a story in John 4. A Samaritan woman encounters Jesus, and her life is completely transformed. Her first reaction is to go back to her village to proclaim what Jesus had done in her life, and as a result, "many Samaritans from the village believed in Jesus" (John 4:39 NLT). The woman did not share an overly complicated message nor utilize some intricate special method. She simply shared her story about Jesus, and many people were captivated.

Paul the apostle did not seem to take an overly complicated approach either. He proclaimed, "I passed on to you what was most important and what had also been passed on to me. Christ died for our sins, just as the Scriptures said. He was buried, and he was raised from the dead on the third day, just as the Scriptures said" (1 Corinthians 15:3-4 NLT).

Paul's message was powerful. So powerful that it changed the entire world. Yet Paul's message was simple: Jesus died for our sins, He was buried, and He rose from the dead!

What if that was the message we proclaimed? What if we simply shared how Jesus changed our lives in the present because of what He did for us in the past?

I wonder if God designed it this way. For the Scriptures declare that Satan "has blinded the minds of the unbelievers, to keep them from seeing the light of the gospel" (2 Corinthians 4:4 ESV), yet Christians have conquered Satan "by the blood of the Lamb and by the word of their testimony" (Revelation 12:11 ESV). We can overcome Satan's strongholds in the world as we declare our testimony—how Jesus has transformed our lives—and as we declare what Jesus has already accomplished on the cross, the simple gospel message. The message of Jesus' death and resurrection declares what He has already done. Our testimony reveals what Jesus is still doing, alive and active in the present tense! This message always has and continues to penetrate and captivate hearts to this day!

If you have met Jesus, you have both the *what* and the *how* of carrying the message of a watchman or watchwoman! Simply share your story of how Jesus has shown up for you or transformed your life!

Here are three *simple* steps in sharing your God story:

1. Share what your life was like before encountering Jesus. What difficulty did you face? What negative things did you experience? What misconceptions did you have about God?

2. Share about how Jesus changed your life. What is now different in your life because of Jesus? What is the real change Jesus has brought? But maybe you're wondering, *What if I believed in Jesus when I was really young and don't have a before/after story?* Your story might be your salvation experience, but it might also be a post-salvation experience when Jesus really showed up for you and changed your heart or circumstances.

3. After you share your story, I encourage you to share the simple gospel message in this practical way: "This was possible in my life because of what Jesus has done for us. Jesus died on the cross for our sins, which separated us from the one true God. Jesus then rose from the dead, so He is alive today and waiting for relationship

with us. Is that something you are interested in? Do you want Jesus to change your life too?"

Now before you take up the cause as God's watchman or watchwoman, consider that a *simple* message doesn't mean an *easy* or *risk-free* task. Revelation 12:11 tells us, "they did not love their lives so much as to shrink from death" (NIV). Those believers were willing to proclaim the message of Jesus even if it cost them their lives! As we proclaim the good news, some of us could face death as God sends us to dangerous places to share Jesus with unreached people around the world. While we must be willing to face death, most of us will not face martyrdom. Most of us will, however, experience hardship, discouragement, rejection, and ridicule.

Such opposition begs the question, how will we stand with such strength and grit?

Back in the Himalayas around the table that night, our friend Aliza had shared one more thing before our long evening of conversation ended. We had asked Aliza, "How did you find the courage to go and share the message, even as people oppose you?"

Aliza joyfully replied, "I began to spend more time with Jesus Himself, in His Word and especially in prayer. As I spent time with Him, I found myself having more courage to go and share."

Aliza did not love her life more than the mission. Neither did she love herself more than the people God had sent her to love. As we go to share the gospel, we must not love our own lives more than the lives of those who are in danger of spending eternity without Christ!

So what are you waiting for? Be the watchman or watch-woman God created you to be. Go and proclaim Jesus' story! Share your story and how Jesus has changed your life. As you do, make it simple. Make it about Jesus and the people He's sent you to love. Expect opposition. Equally, expect God's strength and provision along the way. You have what it takes to courageously share His message. Why? Because the living Jesus will surely go with you, to the very end.

Now What?

- Has Satan tried to overcomplicate the gospel in your life? How so? Have you ever realized that sharing the message of Jesus could be so simple and personal? How do the truths revealed in this chapter change your perspective on evangelism?
- What is your Jesus story? Write it out, practice it a couple times, and begin to share it with anyone and everyone!
- In the next few days, who is one person you can share your simple Jesus story and the simple gospel message with? Pray for them now and prepare to share your Jesus story with them.

EIGHT

THE POWER OF THE MESSAGE

WE WERE FIGHTING traffic as we traveled around the main city of a prominent island in Asia. Our drive became like a giant game of reverse dodgeball, where we became the ball trying to dodge all the other drivers. My wife and I along with our local partners had just returned from interior jungle areas and were headed to meet an organizational leader who provided Christian care and education for children in impoverished families.

A bit frazzled (our make-believe "dodgeball game" feeling a little too real), we finally arrived at the ministry center. The leader and staff warmly greeted us.

"Welcome to our center," the leader said on behalf of all who were there. "We are very happy to have you here!"

"Thank you so much for welcoming us here, brother!"

Turning to the two people standing to his right, the leader said, "I want you to meet one of the students here. This is Naloti and her mother."

"Hello," I said, acknowledging each of them with an affirming head nod. "Nice to meet you both!"

While we talked with the leader about their organization's work, I looked for ways to keep Naloti engaged in the conversation too. At an appropriate break in the conversation, I turned and asked Naloti a question (it's amazing how one question can open the door for significant gospel opportunity):

"So, Naloti, what do you like to do for fun?"

"I like to read Buddhist books," she replied.

I was a bit surprised. I had assumed she was a believer due to the center's Christian foundation.

The country we were in actively restricts Christians from sharing the gospel or making "converts." In fact, it's highly illegal. Knowing this, I certainly didn't want to risk our entire ministry in this single moment. Yet my heart burned with a desire to share Jesus with Naloti. Knowing that her mother could drag us into muddy water if we crossed any legal religious lines, I decided to share about Jesus with her anyway, cautiously.

"You know, Naloti, I used to think that my life dream would satisfy me and bring me peace and purpose. But I discovered that as I spent time with the living Jesus, He satisfied me more than anything else on this planet!" I left it at that to see if what I said resonated with her and how she might respond.

Naloti's mother stepped into the conversation. Her response surprised me. She began sharing about her own life of suffering. "The doctors told me that I had cancer," she said. "Things were not looking good. At the same time, our landlord threatened to evict our family from our home and began making plans toward that end. We prayed and prayed and prayed. We gave our sacrifices at the Buddhist temple, but nothing changed. We hit one of the lowest points in our lives."

"I am so sorry for your difficulty," I replied, leaning in and intently listening as she continued.

"I didn't know what else to do," she continued, "so I decided to go to a church gathering and see if their God could help me. They prayed over me, and my cancer has been gone ever since. The threat of eviction just dropped. I discovered the God who could answer our prayers!

"So, I have decided to believe in Jesus. But my husband is still a Buddhist. Whenever he goes to the temple, I tell him, 'I am not feeling well enough to go. I'll stay back and you go without me.' That excuse works for me, but not for my children. My husband takes my children with him to the temple. So, for now, they do not yet follow Jesus either."

"Thank you for sharing your story," I said affirmingly. "We are so excited to hear how God is answering your prayers. We would love to share more about Jesus with your daughter if that is okay with you."

"Absolutely, please do!" she replied.

Permission granted, we began sharing the story of Jesus with Naloti. We began with creation, the fall, and why Jesus came to Earth. Then we shared how He lived, about His death and resurrection, and how powerful He really is as the King of all, the one true God.

As we shared, Naloti's eyes began rolling into the back of her head and her hands were shaking. It seemed as if the enemy was gripping Naloti's life, launching a final initiative to keep her in the kingdom of darkness. But we were unwilling to let Satan have his way. My wife began quietly praying, and I continued to proclaim the message of Jesus, the good news of His victory!

I asked Naloti, "Would you like to believe in Jesus and follow Him too?"

"Yes, I would," she replied.

Immediately her eyes returned to normal and her body stopped trembling. The Prince of Peace entered the scene. Jesus, as we read about many times in Scripture, had taken charge and calmed the storm. His kingdom of light had begun to shine into Naloti's heart.

"Naloti, if you would like to follow Jesus, just pray out loud in your own words. Tell Jesus you are sorry for your sin. Thank Him for dying for you, and tell Him you believe that He rose from the dead. Tell God that you want to give Him your life."

Naloti prayed that prayer. It was the first conversation with Jesus she'd ever had. When she finished, we prayed over her. It was an unexpected but powerful moment to witness the kingdom of God breaking into our everyday moments.

Naloti and her mother had been experiencing life at unsteady, unreliable, and shakable levels. Their life could crumble in a single moment and strip them of all they knew—their relationship, their home, even their next breath. But as Naloti and her mother laid down their lives, Jesus offered them a life in His unshakable kingdom (Hebrews 12:28).

Naloti experienced the reality of the gospel, the good news about Jesus. She placed her trust in the King of the unshakable kingdom. She believed the very message Jesus Himself proclaimed and asked us to pray for:

> *Jesus went into Galilee, proclaiming* the good news *of God.* "*The time has come,*" *he said.* "*The* kingdom of God has come *near. Repent and believe* the good news!" *(Mark 1:15 NIV, italics mine).*
>
> "*This, then, is how you should pray: 'Our Father in heaven, hallowed be your name,* your kingdom come, *your will be done, on earth as it is in heaven'*" *(Matthew 6:9–10 NIV).*

This is the exact message the followers of Jesus were sent to proclaim as well (Acts 28:31).

And what is the power of this *good news*, the gospel message we're called to proclaim? It's none other than Jesus taking His rightful place as King. His rightful place as King of our lives. His rightful place as King of the universe. His rightful place as King of all things, seen and unseen. His rightful place as King based on the evidence of His life, death, resurrection, and exaltation—that Jesus is King and Lord above all else.

As believers we wrestle against the spiritual forces of evil that have been sent by the ruler of the air, the prince of the kingdom of darkness, Satan himself. We witnessed this reality as light pushed back darkness in Naloti's life. The good news is that Jesus has been victorious! And now His kingdom—where whatever God desires to happen, actually happens—is breaking through the spiritual darkness into our very own lives, and through us to everyone around us.

I like to think of it through the lens of a TV show called *Stranger Things*. When creatures from a dark shadow realm break into the realm of everyday life, a junior high kid is taken captive and transported into that dark realm. As his friends and family seek to rescue him, they discover that the two realms coexist at the same time and sometimes overlap.

In the same way, there is a spiritual realm coexisting with our physical realm, and at times we experience the overlap. There is a constant spiritual battle going on around us in the unseen realm. And God desires to see His kingdom come among us, overcoming the darkness and transforming our everyday lives.

The thing is, due to the fall, we have set ourselves up as kings of our own kingdoms. This is true for all of humanity. We love to lead the charge in whatever we do. We like life to go the way we desire, and we get upset when it doesn't. And as believers, too often we allow that mind-set to creep back in. We become stuck focusing on our visible realm, on our needs and our comforts.

But the Scriptures declare a stronger reality: Christ is our life (Colossians 3:4)! We must look beyond ourselves to Christ, who is seated above all else in the heavenly places! Our lives have been crucified with Christ. It is no longer we who live but Christ who lives in and through us (Galatians 2:20)! We cannot forget: Jesus is King, and His kingdom is coming from His position of authority in the heavenly realms.

Whenever we go to share our testimony or proclaim the basic message of the gospel, we must remember the message that Jesus and His followers proclaimed: the reality of the kingdom of God. They proclaimed another King besides Caesar, one called Jesus (Acts 17:7), and so must we! Our simple testimonies of transformation declare that Jesus is King because they reveal His power to change lives, to instill peace in all circumstances, and to bring joy beyond measure. Our stories reveal that Jesus is alive, active today, and the one with all authority!

The gospel message is truly a revolutionary message of power, hope, and transformation. It is a message that will radically change our lives. And not our lives only, but also entire communities, people groups, and nations! It is a message worth giving our very lives for—everything we have and all that we are. Jesus taking His rightful place as King transformed Naloti's life, her mother's life, and I pray it's changed your life as well.

Jesus desires to transform those around you too. Have you realized the power behind the message that has been proclaimed for more than two thousand years? "Freely you have received," Jesus told his disciples (Matthew 10:8 NIV), so "freely give." Isn't it time to be giving what you've so freely been given?

Now What?

- When was a time you witnessed the power of the gospel?
- Have you ever considered that the message Paul the apostle, the first twelve disciples, and Jesus Himself all proclaimed was the kingdom of God? Why do you think we have often missed that part of the gospel message?
- Jesus' "gospel" message was this: "The kingdom of God has come near. Repent and believe the good news" (Mark 1:15 NIV). Other early believers went proclaiming Jesus is King. The power of this message stirred up entire cities. Knowing this, how might it change the message you proclaim or the way you proclaim it?

NINE

RADICAL SECURITY

I SAT across from my great-uncle. Trevor, my grandfather's brother was visiting the States. Uncle Trevor called England home. While England was his country of origin and place of current residence, Uncle Trevor had spent forty-some years living in India as a missionary. I felt blessed by his visit, and I couldn't wait to ask questions and hear more about his experiences of giving all for the gospel among the unreached in South Asia. I had no doubt that he had some wild stories to tell!

Ready for a lengthy conversation, I jumped in, "So, Uncle Trevor, tell me how you began. Why did you leave England for India?"

Uncle Trevor spoke in a quiet yet confident tone. His speech reflected a man who was content in all circumstances and filled with unspeakable joy. "Well, as you know, your grandfather and I grew up in England," he began. "Our father died in World War I while aboard a naval ship that was bombarded by enemy fire and sank. As a young boy, I remember my brother—your grandpa, Peter—standing guard with a rifle at a military site at the young age of thirteen. One day, Peter told me he saw the entire sky turn black, covered with planes going off to war. We knew what we needed to do. Our father had joined the British Navy, so when the time came, we enlisted too. I was seventeen years old.

"While I was serving in the navy, I fully committed my life to Jesus through the Naval Christian Fellowship. Not long after I happened to meet some missionaries who shared some amazing stories with me. They shared about God calling them to unreached people who had never heard of Jesus and how God has called us as Christians to make disciples of all nations. God began tugging on my heart. I knew He was calling me to unreached people too. The burden was so deep, I knew I had to do something. I also knew some major changes were needed for me to do what God was asking."

"And what was happening with Grandpa Peter at that time?" I asked.

"Your grandpa was also having encounters with the Lord," Uncle Trevor recalled. "One night he came in from the town, drunk, as he often did. But that time I sat down to pray with him. As he sobered up, I was able to share about Jesus and how He was already changing my life."

"Uncle Trevor, that is amazing that God gave you this opportunity to share with your brother. I imagine it prepared him to give his life to Jesus! I remember Grandpa Peter telling me about his salvation moment. He was sailing through the Arctic Circle and was blown off the deck of his deployed ship. Miraculously, nets off the side of the ship caught him as he fell. Still, he was gravely injured. His life was in danger, and clearly his eternal destiny too."

I shifted in my chair and continued, "Grandpa Peter told me that he wasn't a believer at the time. As he recovered in the hospital, however, he shared about reading the Gideon Bible placed beside his bed. Someone saw him reading and explained the good news of Jesus to him. Grandpa Peter told me that he was finally ready to give his life to Christ in that hospital room, and everything changed."

Trevor interjected, "God was certainly at work in your grand-pa's life all along the way. His heart had been impacted and primed for salvation having recently attended a Billy Graham crusade, which would also later compel him to tell others about Jesus every-where he went!"

Our conversation rekindled a memory about my grandfather. "I remember Grandpa Peter jokingly say he was saved by several things: 'God, the Gideon Bible, and Guinness!' He surely had a unique sense of humor, didn't he?!"

Uncle Trevor chuckled. "Yes, he did. Being a proper English-men, he had certainly enjoyed occasional outings to the pub. Apparently, your grandpa thought the iron content of Guinness somehow strengthened his body! And what a brilliant case in point," Uncle Trevor continued, "of how Peter often shared his own quirky combination of God's truth and humor."

I was grateful to God as I recalled the unique ways my grand-father joyfully lived his life to the fullest. He could hardly go anywhere without telling people about Jesus or sharing some portion of Scripture that had gripped him—all the while using his God-instilled gift of dry British humor to break the ice.

"I wish Grandpa Peter was still here," I said to Uncle Trevor, "so I could tell him about all God has done. I remember returning from my first trip to Africa when I was quite young. Grandpa Peter asked me, 'What did God do on your trip?' I began sharing about all that *we* had done—like painting a church and playing with orphans. But Grandpa wanted to know what *Jesus* had done. At the time, I didn't have the spiritual maturity to understand what Grandpa was asking."

I paused, imagining that moment years ago. "Years later, after witnessing all God has done, I finally understand what Grandpa was hungering to hear. He wanted me to share God's stories, God's activity, God's transforming power at work. I know that Grandpa was interested in my life and what I was doing for the kingdom. But Grandpa knew who the real star and headliner was in every story, and it was *His* story Grandpa wanted to hear. I can't wait for us to see him in heaven, Uncle Trevor, so we can all rejoice together for all that Jesus did then and all He continues to do!"

Uncle Trevor grinned ear to ear, "Your grandpa would be so proud of you and all God is doing now!"

I was eager to know more. "So, back to the story, what happened next?" I asked.

"With all God was orchestrating, your grandpa and I were confident God was calling us to leave the British Navy for the mission field. But there was one problem. Our military service commitment wasn't up yet. Certain of God's call and sensing an urgency to embrace it, we asked God for a way forward. He provided one. At that time, you could pay your way out of military service. So, we paid our way out of the British Navy, and along with our wives, we left for missions training through New Tribes Missions in the United States.

"Near the completion of our missions training, your Aunt Rona and I prayerfully discerned God calling us to India. We sought to be sent and supported by our local congregation, which was part of the organized Church of England at the time. Unfortunately, they would not support our endeavor."

Uncle Trevor paused a moment, still baffled all these years later at the congregation's decision. With a sorrowful tone in his voice he continued, "They did not believe in our calling for the nations. So, we ventured out on our own with little support, trusting God would provide for our family and make a way. And you know what? He always has! Aunt Rona and I moved to India while your grandpa trusted God with his kingdom assignment: moving to Wisconsin and starting a Christian camp while running a farm."

I had so many questions and so little time. Wanting to hear more God-glorifying adventures from Uncle Trevor, I asked, "I know you often went to survey unreached areas of India. Can you tell me about one of the most interesting tribal encounters you had?"

Uncle Trevor smiled and kindly obliged. "There was a particular tribe that we felt God wanted us to scout out. Others warned us and said, 'Don't go! They are headhunters. Anytime someone goes there, they are murdered. It is too dangerous!' I replied, 'We will go anyway! We don't need to be afraid. Jesus is with us. And if we die, we will go to heaven! Therefore, we have nothing to lose.'

"So off to the tribe we went. When we arrived in the village, the chief approached me. I wasn't sure what to expect nor what he might say or do. But what happened was far beyond any expectations."

Intrigued and gripped with anticipation, I leaned forward in my chair.

Uncle Trevor continued, "The chief picked me up in his arms and, get this, he began to dance! Not really knowing what to do, I quickly prayed and, after the chief set me down, I felt that I should pick him up and dance too. So that's what I did! Gathering the chief in my arms, I picked him up and danced around. As you can imagine, it was quite the sight! I later discovered that this was a sign of acceptance among the people group. God had opened a door and made a way for us."

People like Uncle Trevor, who give their entire lives for the kingdom cause, amaze me. His life has been consistently marked by contagious joy, quick generosity, constant contentment, and undying passion for seeing the lost meet Jesus. Uncle Trevor has risked his reputation, family, finances, and even his own life.

My uncle, God's ambassador, never seems to worry about what others think of him, where his provision will come from, his potential lack of abilities, his family's safety, or whether he will take another breath. For many, it's so easy to feel insecure, wondering and worrying about such life issues. How could Trevor live in such a way? Where does his confidence come from? I believe Uncle Trevor has intently and passionately embraced the great unknown of life because he has been gripped by a greater reality: radical security. Because Jesus has all authority, we can experience radical security (Matthew 28:18; Ephesians 1:20–21).

People may come against us, our next paycheck may be uncertain, and our inadequacies may overshadow and paralyze us. We may crumble when we listen to the enemy's lies, diversions, and discouragement: *Didn't you mess up last week or even this morning?!*

You don't have what it takes! How can you possibly stand firm when opposition arises? You should be afraid to take another step forward given all the unknowns! Many of us allow our internal battles as well as Satan's whispers to crumble the cause of Christ in our lives.

If you feel this describes you, you aren't alone. In the context of the Great Commission, even the disciples who had just encountered the risen Jesus doubted (Matthew 28:17). And Jesus' response to them was not, "You're right! Your doubts and struggles are too big for me. Make sure you figure them all out before I send you to go make disciples of all nations." No, Jesus told them, "All authority in heaven and on earth has been given to me. Therefore go and make disciples . . ." (Matthew 28:18–19 NIV).

We do not "go make disciples" because we have the exact training, skills, spiritual pedigree, or some special ability to overcome our struggles. We go into all the earth and make disciples because Jesus, the one with all authority, has already spoken, "Go!" His authority is not only big enough to overcome our internal battles and Satan's advances, but more than enough to squelch any amount of resistance that people around us put forth—whether a neighbor, coworker, family member, people group, or an entire nation's restrictive government. God's authority will provide us with everything we need, for every situation.

Whatever may come at us, Jesus holds all authority—in heaven and on Earth (Matthew 28:18). He is definitively and securely in charge. Jesus holds us firmly in His hand, and no one can snatch us from Him (John 10:28). And absolutely nothing we encounter can separate us from Him (Romans 8:39). God is all-sufficient; He provides all we need for life and godliness (2 Peter 1:3). In fact, Jesus Himself is all we need. You can rest assured by that truth. You do not have to be afraid. You can live securely while living radically. You can live a life marked by radical security.

Now What?

- What causes you the greatest insecurity in your life?

Imagine if you didn't have to let insecurities run your life.

- What would it take for you to live with a sense of radical security?
- In light of His authority, what can you specifically do this week to begin living with radical security?

TEN

MOVEMENT MINDED

AT THE END of a forty-five-minute trek up and over the mountain behind her home, Mary entered the village of Mandagow. She regularly ventures to various villages, taking the message of Jesus to those who desperately need it.

On this voyage Mary met two women who were ill and discouraged. One of them shared, "We cannot leave our village due to the extreme pain in our legs. We can barely stand or walk."

"Have you tried any medicine?" Mary inquired.

"Yes, we have tried traditional tribal medicine, and we have even gone to a doctor. Nothing has helped."

Mary moved in with confidence. "Let me pray over you."

Mary fervently sought Jesus, praying, "Lord, will you help these women? I pray that you would heal their legs in the name of Jesus!"

After the "amen," the women looked up and one exclaimed with excitement, "Our legs feel better. And we can walk! God healed us! Nothing has ever worked . . . until now."

Mary seized the moment and immediately began teaching these women about Jesus and what He has done for us. The women needed no convincing; God had already revealed His power. They gave their lives to Jesus that very moment!

Over the next week, Mary trained the women how to live as disciples: by obeying the commands of Jesus out of their love for Him. The two women, although elder in years, began running their races with youthful zeal!

Mary enthusiastically recalled the story. "These women are quite funny actually," Mary explained. "They tell *every* person they see about Jesus. They cannot meet a single person without speaking of Jesus. After a mutual greeting with whoever they meet, they immediately begin to proclaim who Jesus is and how He has worked in their lives!

"And people are genuinely believing in Jesus when these women share their testimonies. Everyone can see the evidence of what God has done—not only in their bodies but also in how He's transformed their lives!"

The message did not end with these two women. God never intended it to. His desire is that the gospel message reach everyone. The two women didn't need prodding. When the "good news" is good news to you, you can't wait to share it with others. That's exactly what the women did. In the time that Mary had begun training her new sisters in the faith, they had already shared the good news with another woman. That woman committed her life to Jesus, and the women began training her in the same way Mary was training them. A mini movement had begun.

Before 2014 the Hadzabe people had no Bible, no church gathering, and no disciple making in their language. Now the Hadzabe have the entire New Testament and much of the Old Testament in their language, evangelism is happening from village to village, and Mary has initiated a local house church gathering along with some others in the area.

Four years after stepping foot among the Hadzabe people, we received an email from an American anthropologist. This anthropologist had been working with the Hadzabe for over ten years and was researching "how religious beliefs may impact certain behaviors such as cooperation and morally good behavior." He stated, "I have conducted hundreds of interviews on Hadza religious beliefs in both 2013 and 2014." But what caught us off guard was this statement tucked in the email: "I have noticed a sharp rise in Christianity." It turns out the researcher emailed us to inquire what we had done to make this possible. God's work among the Hadzabe people confirmed His heart for multiplying movements.

So, how does a movement grow from a spark to a wildfire? How is Jesus' kingdom movement surging forward and expanding?

I believe Paul shares the secret as he writes to Timothy: "The things you have heard me say in the presence of many witnesses entrust to reliable people who will also be qualified to teach others" (2 Timothy 2:2 NIV). Did you catch it? Not one, or two, or three, but four spiritual generations are included in this verse! From Paul to Timothy to "reliable people" to "others." Kingdom movement—not by addition but through multiplication! Paul provides the framework for sparking a movement through spiritual multiplication.

It's the same wisdom my great-uncle learned and passed on to me. "My greatest learning from the mission field is this," Uncle Trevor once told me: "Teach others to do what you cannot do. And even if you can do it, teach them anyway." Uncle Trevor's greatest learning was a perfect reflection of 2 Timothy 2:2.

There is a Jesus movement among the Hadzabe because spiritual multiplication is taking place. No one is attempting to contain the fire. No one is seeking to douse zeal for Jesus. No one is reserving the mission for the "more educated" or "capable." Rather, ordinary people are becoming *radical firestarters* for the kingdom. Like firebrands in a forest fire, they are being sent out by the blowing of the Holy Spirit to share God's message to people and villages all around. And God is igniting hearts and transforming lives!

Mary is not the only one teaching others. She is sending others to do the same. In turn, they are also sending others to do the same. Others training others training others. Anyone who believes in Jesus shares Jesus. And anyone who shares Jesus teaches others to obey Jesus. The Hadzabe have become movement minded.

Those who embrace a movement mind-set witness incredible kingdom transformation multiplied! Spiritual multiplication and multiplying movements aren't limited to the Hadzabe and their story. One individual we equipped in an Asian Muslim country simply began sharing about Jesus daily and equipping others to do the same. In just six months, over six hundred new believers committed their lives to Jesus—new believers spanning ten spiritual generations and meeting together in ten house churches.

There's a joy that comes in multiplying others. A joy that comes in fulfilling God's mission. A joy from seeing peace and contentment on a new believer's face. And a joy knowing that, when empowered, the feet of multiplying mudrunners will take the gospel to places our feet never will, impacting people we could never reach.

I will never forget the day when a cleaning lady approached me as I sat reading my Bible in a hotel lobby. She excitedly pointed at my Bible.

"Hola, you read Bible!" the woman said in broken English. Neither of us knew each other's language well enough to really converse, so I opened the Google Translate app on my phone to see if we could have a simple conversation.

I spoke into my phone, "Yes, I am reading the Bible! Are you a Christian?" Instantly and somewhat magically, a Spanish voice spoke out of my phone (although with a robotic accent).

"Yes, I am a believer," my phone mechanically declared after the woman spoke into my phone, grinning ear to ear.

"What is your name?" I inquired of my new friend.

"My name is Maria."

I couldn't help but think, *The way Maria so joyfully reached out to a stranger reading the Bible makes me believe she really loves Jesus.* I had a sense that Maria's life was a bright light to many, so I took the conversation a little deeper. "Maria, as I have walked around and spent time here, I feel like this place is spiritually dark. You are a bright light in a dark place. Thank you for your daily ministry to everyone you encounter."

"Muchas gracias, muchas gracias," Maria said, in words I could actually translate myself.

"Can I pray for you?" I offered.

"Of course."

I laid my hand on Maria's shoulder and prayed in English without any translation. As I finished praying, I looked up. Tears filled Maria's eyes and streamed down her cheeks. She grabbed my phone and declared through Google Translate, "Thank you so much for praying. It means so much to me. I want you to know, today I will share Jesus with the entire hotel staff!"

I was both shocked and amazed at the power of God in such a simple moment. I had prayed for God's impact in Maria's life and for His kingdom movement through her life. The Spirit of God seemed to burn my prayer into her heart! I would never be able to reach the entire hotel staff, nor would I even know how to begin. But Maria could and declared she would! You never know how far a small act will go to spur on a movement.

I believe movement-minded living is what Jesus intended for every believer when He commissioned us to "go and make disciples of all nations" (Matthew 28:19 NIV). While Jesus knew not every believer would step foot in every nation, even still He casts a wild vision of disciples making disciples among every ethnolinguistic people group on the planet—here, there, and everywhere. Making disciples of all nations requires some serious multiplication of movement-minded Jesus lovers. We must continually multiply others if we really are serious about accomplishing Jesus' vision of reaching the remaining unreached regions of the world.

Now What?

- What would living with a movement mind-set look like in your context?
- Who is one person you can begin to invest your time

in right now, equipping them to obey Jesus, and then training them to go and do the same?

- Go to MultiplyingMovements.com and check out the "Discipleship Tool for Everyday Followers of Jesus," designed to equip mudrunners like yourself to spiritually multiply others for God's kingdom movement!

ELEVEN

FLASHPOINT OPPORTUNITIES

JUST OUTSIDE MARY'S two-room mud-brick house in East Africa, Nathan, Bai, and I sat down in wobbly wooden chairs as Mary prepared cups of *chai* for us. I looked across the table at Bai. He was quiet and soft-spoken. He appeared to have a sense of inner strength while equally struggling with a deeper inner turmoil.

I casually began conversation by asking, "So, Bai, where are you from?"

"My family is from the main city," he replied, "but I came out to the bush for work."

The obvious follow-up question spilled from my lips: "What do you do for work?"

"I am a farmer, and I also work in the mines not too far from here," he said matter-of-factly.

Mary poured the chai. We took a few sips and continued our conversation. I felt God desired us to go deeper.

"Bai, are you born again?" I asked. (On a quick side note: in East Africa, the term "born again" is used to describe committed followers of Jesus, while the term "Christian" often equates to only having knowledge *about* Jesus while lacking relationship with Him).

"No," Bai replied. His tone suggested the inner turmoil I sensed in him. He continued, "How could God care about me? We are going hungry! We work hard on the farm, but our crops are not doing well. There is not enough rain. We are suffering. How could God possibly care about us while this is happening?"

"I am so sorry for your difficulty," I replied with a heavy heart. "Jesus cares so much for you. I believe He is even weeping with you in your suffering."

Bai sat forward, listening intently.

"And Bai," I continued, "Jesus promises He will give you everything you need if you trust Him! He will provide for you. In Matthew 6:33, Jesus says, "Seek first the kingdom of God . . . and all these things will be added to you" (ESV).

Nathan jumped in. "Bai, let me tell you how much He cares for you. In the beginning God created everything we see!"

Nathan picked up some dirt and blew into it with excited animation, adding, "And God breathed into the dust to create man, and it was all good. But as humans, we chose to sin and disobey God, so we were separated from Him. So, God sent His son Jesus to Earth, and Jesus died on the cross to pay for our sins. Then He rose from the dead. And now if we believe, we can have a friendship with Jesus! Jesus totally changed my life, and He can change yours, too, Bai."

Our new friend was taking it all in.

"So, Bai, what do you think?" I asked. "Do you want to trust God and begin a friendship with Jesus? Jesus doesn't want you to struggle alone. He wants to do life with you."

"Yes, I do want to. I am ready to commit my life to Jesus," Bai said earnestly. And right then and there, over a cup of chai, Bai prayed to begin a life with His Lord and Savior, Jesus Christ.

We had no idea how quickly this spark would burst into flame. One week later Bai shared some unexpected news with us. "Darkness has always tormented me and paralyzed me with fear," he explained. "I never sleep well because horrifically frightening nightmares have always plagued my mind, even as a grown man. But Jesus has changed everything! After I prayed to follow Jesus, all the darkness completely disappeared. I am now sleeping like a baby!"

We rejoiced with him. "Bai, that is incredible!" I said. "Jesus is amazing, isn't He?"

"Yes, and I have also been reading the Bible this week. I was really touched by the story where Jesus healed a leper on the Sabbath and the religious leaders became angry. I now realize that Jesus can heal anyone, anywhere, at any time. While the religious leaders really cared about specific days, they forgot about the actual people. Jesus didn't forget. He really cared for the people." He looked at us for confirmation as he asked, "Am I understanding this correctly?"

"Yes, you are getting it perfectly! The Spirit of God is clearly teaching you already, brother," I affirmed.

I was so moved by how much Bai was already beginning to understand. Jesus was already revealing His heart to Bai in palpable and powerful ways. And God has continued to write His kingdom story in and through Bai's life.

Our encounter with Bai was not a planned ministry event. We were simply sitting and drinking a cup of tea. Nothing notable or extraordinary was on the calendar that day as we spent time sipping chai around Mary's table. But Jesus turned our everyday minutes into a kingdom moment in Bai's life!

I love how Paul, the writer of Colossians, puts it: "Walk in wisdom toward outsiders, making the best use of the time" (Colossians 4:5 ESV). In the Greek language and culture of Paul's day, there were two words to convey the concept of time: *kairos* and *chronos*. *Chronos* can simply be understood by a ticking clock or a calendar. Seconds tick, minutes pass, days come and go, and months turn to years. Time keeps on moving chronologically and cannot be stopped. On the other hand, *kairos* is more like a match bursting into flame, or a flashpoint. It is a special breakthrough kind of moment in time.

I find it interesting that Kairos was the name of a Greek god who had a frizzy rod of hair on the front of his head but was bald on the back. It was said that when this god came near a person, they could grab ahold of his crazy hair to seize the moment. But if this god passed by a person, they would never get that moment back again. The moment would be gone forever because no one could grab the back of Kairos's bald head as he slipped on by. I imagine that his head must have been spit-shined!

Kairos happens to be the word Paul uses in this specific verse. Seize the moment among outsiders! Make the best use of the time! Don't let it pass on by! It's crucial that we grab ahold of potential kingdom moments in the midst of our everyday minutes, or those opportunities may pass by and never return.

When we move too quickly and run too frantically—living as tunnel-visioned, timid, afraid, or self-absorbed people—we often miss opportunities right in front of us, opportunities we risk never getting back.

Now, check this out: it is noteworthy that Paul tells us, "*Walk in wisdom*" (Colossians 4:5 ESV, italics mine). If we run too fast too soon, it will be difficult to make it to the finish line. Sometimes we need to slow our running for the sake of the long game and finishing well. At times, our running might look a bit more like speed walking as we pause to take inventory of what's right in front us. At any rate, it's important, as we run, to move at God's pace under the direction of His Spirit.

Jesus wants to turn our everyday minutes into moments for His kingdom, appointed moments often outside our previously scheduled plans. The race we are running is often full of unseen opportunities—opportunities that may be waiting in the form of the next person sitting across from you at a lunch table, in line at a grocery store, in a chat on social media, or on a collaborative project for school or work. It's likely that the next person you encounter is meant for more than casual conversation. Every encounter, daily event, and casual exchange is ripe for significant kingdom conversation. Will you slow your pace enough to look past your *minutes* to the potential *moments* God may have for you? Doing so will actually advance God's kingdom further, faster, and give you the assurance that you haven't missed a thing God has for you along the way.

Now What?

- Are you currently more driven by your calendar, plans, and the busy demands of life, or by God's agenda? How so?
- What are some places in your everyday life that you might be overlooking potential kingdom moments?
- Starting this week, what will you do to remind yourself to look beyond your minutes to seize-able kingdom moments?

TWELVE

ENGULFED IN DARKNESS

SINCE I BEGAN RUNNING the race for the cause of Christ, I have experienced some of the best days of my life—and some of the worst. The day I'm about to tell you about was among the worst.

Mahee-uh, a tribal villager, came to us and asked, "Will you take my daughter to the hospital? She is sick."

Mary and Nathan gathered with me to pray and seek the Lord's direction on what to do. We wanted to be good stewards of God's time and resources. Saying yes to every request in places like East Africa can rather quickly turn you into an ambulance or taxi driver.

"Lord, what do you want us to do?" we prayed.

"Wait" is what all three of us felt was God's direction as we prayed.

Adding to the confirmation was the information that an African doctor in the area had already given the girl some sort of medicine. So, we waited.

Three days later, a tribal member stormed into our campsite. His chest pounding, panic filled his eyes. His voice quaked as he managed to verbalize what he came to tell us: "Follow me!"

We quickly got up and followed him as we made the two-minute run through the bush. Mahee-uh was on his knees, cradling his daughter, Joyce, in his arms. She was going in and out of consciousness and coughing up blood. We had to do something. We could not just sit back and watch Joyce die!

We grabbed our backpacks containing essential travel gear and packed into our small Suzuki sedan. The hospital was a several-hour journey away. I drove as quickly as I possibly could while trying to avoid deep potholes and weaving around large rocks that would surely puncture our gas tank (lessons I had already learned the hard way a time or two).

When we arrived at the hospital, the doctors moved far slower than the urgency our hearts beat with, which we perceived was necessary for Joyce's situation. We tried to be patient. After all, we were not the doctors, and this was not our homeland. They laid Joyce on a bed and began to check her vital signs. The doctors continued to walk in and out as they attended to other patients. Meanwhile, Joyce's hands grew colder and colder. Much quicker than the car ride that got her there, Joyce's body went limp. She was gone.

Mahee-uh collapsed over Joyce's lifeless body. He began weeping uncontrollably as agonizing shrieks pierced the deafening silence. I quietly prayed. I had no clue what to do. What could I say? What could I do to ease Mahee-uh's loss and grief? No words would suffice.

We carried Joyce's body back to the car. The silent ride back to the village seemed twice as long as our journey out. Arriving at the village, the black of night matched the shadows that darkened our hearts. Tribal members from every direction began making their way to the car to see what happened. As soon as their eyes caught ours, they knew. Their mournful shrieks rang out as Mahee-uh's had done. They were grieving with him and for him.

Mahee-uh spoke up. "I have been staying at Kiula's home. We can lay Joyce's body there." Now, Kiula's hut was separated from the rest of the village. Past conflicts between Kiula and the rest of the village made the distance necessary. At present, tensions had subsided and were at least tolerable.

As the procession headed toward Kiula's hut, however, he yelled out, "No! Don't bring the body to my house. Everyone always puts their problems on me!"

They crowd was enraged! They immediately began picking up rocks to stone Kiula to death. Taken off guard, I stepped back toward the car. Hostility surged, and the potential for extreme violence escalated, and quick! An African pastor-friend who was on mission with us made his way through the pushing and shoving, and separated the crowd from Kiula. Eventually, everyone calmed down enough to drop their rocks, and Kiula wandered back to his hut.

Mahee-uh spoke again. "Okay fine. We can put the body over at the huts on the other side of the village."

We drove to the other huts and laid Joyce's body on the cold, hard ground. The villagers gathered around. Still angry about Kiula's decision, they began ridiculing him in their stylistic, rapid back-and-forth, cutting conversation.

After a time, I interrupted the group. "I agree with you all. Kiula is wrong. He should have let you put the body at his house. But I need to ask you something. You all said you want to follow Jesus, right?"

"Yes, we did," they replied, some nodding in agreement.

I continued, "We shared with you that Jesus died to forgive your sins, and that He teaches us to forgive others in the same way that He has forgiven us. Therefore, you must forgive Kiula for this terrible action." They nodded in silent agreement.

"Mahee-uh, we want to give you a gift. We know that you lost your first wife, Joyce's mother, and now have lost that blood line as a result. And we know that you would like to bury Joyce with her mother. In the morning, we will drive you to your home village to make this possible."

He thanked us. After a long and draining day, we each made our way to bed.

At daylight, we crammed into the small Suzuki sedan for one

of the worst drives of my life. I drove and Nathan sat in the passenger seat. In the back was Mary, our African pastor-friend, Mahee-uh, and his wife . . . and Joyce's body lying across their laps. Within seconds of pulling away from the huts, a sickening odor filled the car. Joyce's body had already beginning decomposing in the heat. I rolled down the window and muttered a prayer. The long trip was off to a rough start. We had to four-by-four up mountain trails cluttered with sizable rocks. My poor vehicle choice was quickly evident; the Suzuki was not designed for such intense off-roading! I wondered if we might break down or, worse, get stranded in the middle of the bush and never make it to Mahee-uh's home village at all.

Despite the difficulty in navigating the rough terrain of the makeshift bush "roads" for half a day, we made it to the village (most assuredly through mustard seed prayers and God's grace!). Some of the village women took Joyce's body and prepared it for burial. They cleaned the body and wrapped it in white cloth. Meanwhile, we joined the men in digging Joyce's grave. Although we each took turns, every one of us was drenched in sweat by the time we finished.

While we were digging, commotion began stirring in the village.

I inquired, "What is going on?"

"Someone has cut off a certain piece of Joyce's body for witchcraft. They are arguing and trying to find out who did it."

Just when we thought that these two days could not be any darker, darkness seemed to engulf us. As the common expression goes, "When it rains, it pours." We found ourselves thick in the mud puddles of human depravity, and we were in deep. Only through the light of Jesus Christ could there be hope for such a time as this!

Calmer voices prevailed, and the witchcraft dispute was settled, at least enough to start the ceremony. Soon after, everyone gathered together. During the ceremony, tribal leaders asked us to speak. I stood, my heart heavy.

Knowing that only the message of Jesus could bring good out

of such darkness, I spoke up. "We are so sorry for the death of Joyce," I said. "This is a terrible tragedy. Our hearts are in so much pain with you."

As I continued, I declared the gospel of Jesus Christ. Jesus—the one who took on death—rose from the dead and proved His power over death! Jesus is the only solid hope our world has. As I ended the message, I invited the village to put their hope in Jesus, the one who holds power over death. Many people responded. They believed in Jesus and said yes to Him for the first time! At last, a glimpse of hope, a shimmer of light, and a breath of fresh air emerged. Light began to push back the darkness.

I still can't answer why Joyce had to die, nor do I fully understand. It is hard to describe the feeling I sat with, wondering over and again if there was something we could have done differently that would have prevented Joyce from dying. Three things were true: we did our best to follow God's guidance, we waited, and Joyce lost her life. While such tensions are difficult to hold all at the same time, I believe God can be trusted in them all.

I also wrestled with Joyce's destiny, not knowing with certainty where she will spend eternity. But what I do know is this—Joyce heard the good news before she died. Her family heard the good news. Her death provided an opportunity for us to show up in an unreached village, love them in tangible ways, and proclaim the message of Jesus. And on that day, many in the village gave their lives to Christ!

And I know this with even more certainty: God brought life out of death. While physical death visited Mahee-uh's family that day, we witnessed spiritual life infiltrate death and darkness. Jesus victoriously shone through the death, destruction, and darkness of their village for His kingdom purposes. The Gospel of John says it this way: "The light shines in the darkness, and the darkness has not overcome it" (John 1:5 ESV). As with the people in the prophet Isaiah's day, the village can now say, "[We,] the people who walked in darkness have [now] seen a great light" (Isaiah 9:2 ESV). They had now been delivered from lifelong slavery to the fear of death (Hebrews 2:15)!

Having begun the race, have you encountered darkness yet? I imagine you have. But if not, you will. And when you do, be assured of this reality: light shines far brighter in darkness. The darkness provides opportunity for His light to shine all the brighter in your life.

God has ultimately brought life out of death through the cross of Christ. And if God brought life out of death in Mahee-uh's village, He can certainly bring life out of death wherever you may step foot. When you are engulfed in the mud puddles of human depravity and desperation is all around, don't forget that our God brings life out of death and light in the midst of darkness! Light is around the corner. Hold on! Embrace the mud. Endure!

Now What?

- When was a time you faced unimaginable difficulty, darkness, or the depravity of humanity?
- Did you see any glimpses of Christ's light in that situation? How so? If not yet, continue to cling to Christ—His light will ultimately prevail!
- How does knowing that our God brings life out of death shift your perspective on life, darkness, and difficulty?

THIRTEEN

OUR RUNNING GUIDE

"WAS THAT ME OR GOD? I guess we'll find out!" That was my reaction to the bold words that had flashed in my mind. A friend and I were praying in preparation for a trip to an unreached tribe on a prominent island country in South Asia. As we put together a game plan for the trip, I said, "Let's pray and ask Jesus if He has anything to show us."

I had been reading various articles about this specific unreached tribal people as God continued burdening my heart for them. As we prayed, "Jesus, do you have anything specific You want us to do there?" these thoughts immediately flashed in my mind and weighed on my heart: "Find Chief Saduwara Wanujitha. He is searching for more. I want him."

Try saying "Saduwara Wanujitha" five times fast! I remembered having read about this chief as I researched the trip. The chief didn't seem nearly as important then, but having his name come up in prayer boosted his priority. I knew if God really wanted us to find him, we would.

We set off on the journey and arrived as scheduled at our island country destination. Meeting up with some local partners, we discussed where we might be able to find Chief Saduwara

Wanujitha. One of the partners unfolded a map, pointed his finger toward the center, and told us, "You will find this chief and tribe in this general region."

After a full day's drive, we showed up in the region. We began asking around, "Do you know where this man lives? Where can we find his village?"

"Yes, he is that way," one of the locals said with his arm stretched out and finger pointing down the road. We thanked him and continued our search.

Not far down the road, we met another man. He was a pastor whose heart was also burdened in reaching the unreached. Crazy enough, he had interacted with the tribe we were zeroed in on. Clearly, the Spirit of God had brought him across our path!

After guiding us further, the pastor left us with a warning: "Be careful with evangelism in this area. Persecution is strong. We have been poisoned and received death threats. People might beat you and call the local monks to hold you down until the police show up to arrest you. So be careful."

We took note of the pastor's warning but knew we had to continue. We believed God had specifically directed us to meet Chief Saduwara no matter what it might cost us—whatever the path, whatever the danger.

The next day, we reached the chief's village. One of the villagers directed us to where he lived. With anxious excitement and expectation, we drove down the dirt road leading up to his home. As we approached, a woman came out to greet us. We asked her, "Is the chief here?"

The woman told us, "I am his wife, but he is not here now. He is out for the day and will be returning later."

The news was a bit disappointing, but it did give us time to spend a few minutes with the chief's wife and children and grab some lunch in a nearby town.

We returned a couple of hours later. Chief Saduwara had already arrived back home and was waiting for us. The chief was a well-statured man, five feet two inches tall at best. He had brown shiny skin and a scraggly beard that grew wildly, blurring the distinction between where his hair ended and his beard began. He appeared to be gentle and welcoming, his eyes soft and inviting.

We extended our hands with gifts as we greeted him. "We have brought these things to bless your family and your children," I said. "We came from America to meet you. Are we able to talk with you now?"

"I am sorry," he apologized, "but I actually need to leave again."

I wouldn't give up that easily, so I pressed further: "Can we talk for just a few minutes?"

Pondering the time he could afford, he responded, "Yes, we can talk for five or ten minutes before I leave."

I often say, "In missions—and in all of life as a Christian—you have to wait ten hours for a ten-minute moment of ministry." This interaction with the chief certainly seemed to be one of these "ministry" moments. Feeling the urgency of the clock, I thought, *If God led us to this man, we must seize this opportunity and make the most of the time we've been given. It's time to dive right in!*

With no time to waste, I asked, "Chief Saduwara, what is your way of worship?"

"I worship our tribal god. We give sacrifices at his stone statue in our village," he replied.

If the Spirit of God had truly led us to Chief Saduwara and told us that he was searching for more, now was the time to find out. I asked him, "Chief Saduwara, do you feel like in your heart you are searching for something more?"

"Yes I do," he affirmed, "I do feel like I am searching for something more than I have now."

With urgent excitement, I proclaimed, "I believe God has sent us to tell you what you are searching for!"

Chief Saduwara leaned forward intently.

"In the beginning, God created everything we see. He made the sky, trees, plants, and even our food. He then created humanity—man and woman. This God was different than other gods you know of, because He actually walked and talked with the man and woman. But one day, they disobeyed what God had told them to do. Their disobedience really hurt God's heart, and they were cast out from God's presence. They were now separated from their relationship with the living God.

"From this point on, the effects of sin entered the world—death, sickness, disease, war and conflict, division, and suffering. But this was not the end. This God loved humanity so much that He came to Earth to take on the full penalty of sin for humanity. His name is Jesus. He died on a cross for all of our sins and rose from the dead, showing His power over even death itself.

"If you follow Jesus, He will give you peace and joy like you have never had before. Jesus lives in me by His spirit, and I talk with Him every day. I have seen him do powerful things! My father almost died from a horrible allergy to bee stings, but I saw Jesus heal him when we prayed. I know that Jesus is alive today! And I know Jesus desires friendship with us, with you. All you must do is this: stop worshipping all other gods. Begin worshipping and following Jesus alone, the one true God. What do you think of this message?"

The chief said, "I like the message of Jesus, I think it's good."

I moved in closer and asked, "So are you wanting to follow Jesus then?"

"It is difficult to give up my cultural god because I am a chief here," Chief Saduwara said softly as he cast his eyes downward.

"I understand that following Jesus can be a difficult decision," I replied. "I had something in my life that I strongly valued more than anything else, and Jesus asked me to give it up for Him. I promise you, Chief Saduwara, if you decide to follow Jesus, it will be worth it. He will satisfy you."

Knowing our time was coming to a close, I asked, "Are we free to return in the future and discuss more with you?"

"Yes," he said, "you are welcome to return here again."

Chief Saduwara was simply a man pursued by Jesus and searching for more than he had been given. God's hand was clearly at work and undoubtedly evident as displayed in Chief Saduwara's openness to discussing the gospel—especially in such a strong place of persecution and among a people of such strong resistance.

As we walked back to our car, the brother in Christ who had been translating shared what he experienced: "I could really sense the Holy Spirit working while we talked with the chief," he said. "That was amazing!" The Spirit of God really was moving!

Our encounter with Chief Saduwara reminds me of the story in Acts 8:26–40 where the Spirit of God tells a man named Philip to journey down a road. As Philip walks in obedience to the Lord, he sees a chariot on the road. The Spirit of God directs Philip, "Go over and join this chariot." So, Philip does.

It so happens that the man in the chariot was reading a passage in Isaiah that pointed directly to the message of Jesus. The man in the chariot, like Chief Saduwara, was searching for more. And Philip declared what *more* the man was searching for: the good news about Jesus.

As I read the Scriptures, I see a vivid and exciting reality—those who lived as God's mudrunners were led by the Holy Spirit. They heard His voice. They experienced His promptings. They stepped out in faith and did whatever God asked.

Have you ever asked Jesus to speak to you and simply listened for His voice? Have you heard from Him recently? Have you felt His promptings and obeyed?

Since Jesus is truly alive and active today, we can be assured He is still speaking and leading His people. After Jesus rose from the dead and ascended to heaven at the end of the Gospels, He continued speaking throughout the book of Acts and beyond! God has always been a speaking God—from creation to the prophets to Jesus Himself. And how much more now that His Spirit dwells inside us! God is certainly near to us, to our ears, hearts, and minds, delivering the words we need to hear. We only need to listen and obey.

Now, you might be thinking, *Maybe Charlie just ate some bad pizza last night and now has wild pizza visions!* When I manage to miraculously convince my wife that pizza is our best dinner choice, that might occasionally be true. Pizza aside, we cannot deny the reality that God truly desires to guide us daily. Of course, we must remember His voice will always match what He has already spoken in His written Word, the Bible. The Holy Spirit will never contradict what God has already declared in the final authority of the Scriptures.

Why not spent a few minutes in prayer right now. Ask, *Holy Spirit, do you have anything to say to me? Guide me. I will follow.*

It's quite simple: listen and do. And as the Holy Spirit guides you, be prepared for some wild kingdom adventures!

Now What?

- Up to this point in your life, how have you understood God's voice or the ways God communicates with us?
- Consider these common ways that God speaks to us (seen throughout Scripture). Have you experienced any of these? **The Bible:** God always communicates to us through the plain meaning of Scripture and also through Scripture penetrating our hearts based on our specific circumstances. **Whispers:** The still small voice of God often comes in thoughts that are not our own but from the Holy Spirit. **Pictures:** Dreams as we sleep or visions that we see while awake, almost as if they are in our imagination, can be from God. **Burdens:** You may feel heavyhearted or compelled by God that you *must* do something.
- Grab a journal. Pray, asking the Lord in Jesus' name to silence your flesh and the enemy. Ask God to speak to you. Maybe you have a specific question, or maybe you just want to ask if He has anything to say to you. Listen. Write down whatever comes to mind. Confirm it aligns with the teaching of the Bible. Receive it, and when applicable, commit to obey it.

FOURTEEN

THE POWER OF PRAYER

I HAVE WITNESSED the power of specific prayers and watched God answer enough times to know that He does more than we ask or imagine. One particular season absolutely astounded me as God answered prayer after prayer after prayer. I continued to seek Jesus, pray specific bold prayers as I felt led, and watch Him come through.

God answered prayers such as these: praying for nine people to be saved on my birthday (which He answered while I was preaching at a camp. I gave an invitation to follow Jesus and nine people responded. In fact, a "random" woman who happened to walk off the street and into the service was among those nine who gave their lives to Jesus!); praying for God to hold back the rain while we packed up a campsite (the rain ceased until the last item was packed up); and praying for God to provide a person of peace among an unengaged, unreached people group living where the Middle East meets Asia (yep, He did it). God answered each of these prayers with precision! And then there was the time I walked the streets of an impoverished Muslim community in West Africa and prayed continually, *Lord, bring the fruit of salvation in this place.* Soon after praying that prayer, I was joyfully shocked to watch an African brother in Christ lead an old Muslim man and his family to Jesus!

God has certainly increased my faith in undeniable ways through answered prayer. As always, faith has room to grow, and God was providing an opportunity for me to trust Him once again. Ever since we visited Chief Saduwara, the influential leader God led us to on a prominent Asian island country, we had been praying for him. In fact, we had been praying for him for three years—that God would grip his heart and multiply disciples through his life. Now, three years later, God was answering our prayer and making a return trip possible.

Waiting three years for a return visit is not the most logical strategy in getting a disciple-making movement kicked off. Mission textbooks would probably advise differently. Yet this was how the Lord seemed to be leading. Over time, we've learned to trust God's instruction more than our conventional wisdom and timing.

So we traveled back to the chief's home with anticipation and excitement. This time we knew where we were going. We didn't need to waste any time wandering around and asking for directions. After driving all day through the middle of the island, we arrived in Chief Saduwara's region. We drove down the dirt road to his house and stepped out into the humid jungle heat. We greeted each other with smiles and joy. We were so delighted to be reunited. After catching up on life for a while and sharing some gifts with the chief and his family, it was time to take the conversation a step further.

"Do you remember our conversation three years ago?" I asked.

"Yes, I remember," the chief replied.

I wondered, *Had he been processing as I had been praying? Did he actually remember?* I had to ask more.

"So what are you thinking about it?"

"I think our gods must be equal," he concluded.

My heart sunk for a moment as I realized the chief still didn't understand that Jesus was the one true God. A sense of urgency rose within me to seize the moment and take it deeper.

"That is an interesting thought," I replied. "Many people say that all gods are equal. But Jesus claimed to be the one with all authority, to be the only true path, and the one true God. So there is no way that they could actually be equal."

A brother in Christ from another city who had been traveling with us jumped into the conversation and began to share his story. He told of how he was suicidal, attempting to take his own life before he knew the Lord. But followers of Jesus shared the good news with him, and he decided to believe. That day he was saved both physically and spiritually. This brother had an incredibly powerful story. I thought, *Surely it must be touching Chief Saduwara's heart!*

We continued our conversation with Chief Saduwara. We shared how Jesus rising from the dead really makes all the difference. "If Jesus did not rise," we explained, "then what He said doesn't really matter. But if Jesus did rise, then *everything* He said *really, truly* matters!"

Feeling like God was leading, I began to share more than I typically would in a tribal setting. "Many experts of history agree that Jesus was a real man who lived, died on a cross, and then his tomb was found empty three days later," I explained. "His followers went from being in absolute despair over His death to becoming bold proclaimers of His resurrection. They went out into the very city that Jesus was killed and began to proclaim that He had risen from the dead. No one found the body and brought it forth to prove otherwise. All of His followers were willing to die for what they proclaimed—and people do not die for a lie they create themselves.

"So, looking at the evidence, many experts who do not believe in Jesus say that His followers must have all had hallucinations. But by definition, a hallucination is limited to an individual's mind. Two separate people cannot have the same hallucination. Not even the best drugs will do that. Therefore, I believe the best answer is that Jesus really did rise from the dead and is alive today. And as we have told you, our lives have been transformed by Him too!"

The chief intently listened, occasionally nodding his head.

"So, what do you think of all this?" I asked.

"I have concluded that Jesus is God."

"That is a great conclusion!" I exclaimed. "Are you ready to follow Jesus?"

"Yes! I am ready!"

Rejoicing with and for him, I said, "That is so exciting. Let's pray together! Tell Jesus that you believe He died for your sins and rose from the dead. Tell Him you believe in Him, desire to give Him your life, and plan to follow Him."

In that moment, Chief Saduwara prayed and began a relationship with the one, true, living God! Joy immediately filled my heart—and his! My three-year prayer had been answered.

"Welcome to the family," I said with a jubilant smile. "We are now brothers because of Jesus."

"Thank you!" he said. His words reflected a lighter, freer, contented tone.

"And you know what," I added, "I have always really liked you because of that long beard you have! I have been growing mine out recently as well."

The chief smiled, and we laughed together.

I pray that God raises up Chief Saduwara to become a strong spiritual leader among his people and begins to multiply others through him. I also pray that the Lord of the harvest raises up more mudrunners among all the people groups of the world that are currently 0 percent Christian. And even further, I pray that God does this in our lifetime. Will you join me in praying for this? God is in the business of answering specific prayers, and I believe specific prayers are close to the heart of Jesus!

The Scriptures tell a story about a time when Jesus answers a blind man who boldly and specifically calls out to Him (Luke 18:35–43). When Jesus was passing by, the blind man called out, "Jesus, son of David, have mercy on me!" (Luke 18:38 ESV). The crowd tried to shut him up. The blind man wouldn't be silent, he couldn't be—it was too important. He called out even louder, "Son of David, have mercy on me!" (Luke 18:39 ESV).

After he called out the second time, Jesus asked the man to be brought to Him. Jesus asked him, "What do you want me to do for you?" (Luke 18:41 ESV).

The man shares his request, and Jesus gives him all he asks for and more! Note, however, it is only after the blind man gets *specific* with his request that Jesus answers. It's then that the blind him receives his sight and begins walking and leaping, praising God.

Take note: too many of our prayers resemble the blind man when he first called out to Jesus. His request was general and vague: "have mercy." Too many of us, too often, leave our requests right there and never take our prayer life further. Now, on one hand, there's nothing wrong with prayers like, "Lord, have mercy." They are within the character and desire of Jesus, God honors them, and answers them. That said, we may never recognize God's answers to vague prayers. And I believe God has so much more for us! So, Jesus takes us a step further.

Jesus prompts the blind man to get specific: "What do you want me to do for you?" I can almost hear Jesus adding the word *specifically*.

Why would Jesus do that? I don't think it was coincidental. Jesus intentionally desired to cut to the heart of the matter with those He engaged. Could it be that Jesus' question would cause the blind man to engage the deeper, more intimate parts of his life than he would have otherwise? Could it be that Jesus wanted him to consider his request more deeply: "What is it that you are really seeking? And why are you seeking it?"

And what if God interacts with us the same way? What if God desires us to share more specific requests with Him so that we begin to truly process, "What am I really seeking and why?" And what if God really does desire to blow our minds by answering specific requests in ways that build our faith, cause us to faithfully follow Jesus, and perhaps go walking and leaping and praising God all along the way as we proclaim, "Look what God did!"

I believe this is exactly the kind of God we serve! I have witnessed too many specific answers to bold prayers to believe otherwise. What if, starting today, you began to pray specifically rather than vaguely? What God-sized things might God accomplish in and through you?

Set aside some time with Jesus to pray specifically. Ask the Holy Spirit to help you as you evaluate what you are really seeking after. Ask Him to align your heart with His desires for you. Then begin to pray bold and specific prayers. Don't hold back. Write them down, continue to pray them, and wait for God to work!

Now What?

- Do specific prayers scare you? Why or why not?
- Is there anything holding you back from praying bold, specific prayers? What might that be?
- Can you think of any times you have seen God answer specific prayer? If so, how did those moments build your faith? Looking forward, what specific prayers will you begin to seek God for, starting this week?

FIFTEEN

MUDSLINGERS

AS WITH EVERY NEW BELIEVER, Chief Saduwara's decision to believe in Jesus required follow-up if he was going to be trained to obey Jesus and become a faithful follower. Nationals followed up various times, and I made a return trip within two months. As swiftly as we could, we arrived in Saduwara's region to spend time talking about what life with Jesus looks like.

Each day with Saduwara looked like this: arrive at his home, enjoy some time talking and catching up, share a story from God's Word, ask questions and discuss the meaning of the Scriptures shared, give Saduwara a practical challenge for that day, and allow him to ask any clarifying questions.

Our time together with Saduwara brought affirmation to his salvation and provided a firm foundation as a follower of Jesus. He became equipped to share Jesus with his community, learned how to pray, discovered how to spend time with God daily, and received training on how to gather together with believers.

The Spirit of God was working powerfully in Saduwara day by day. As we sat down with Saduwara for one of our daily meetings, he declared, "I have already told several others in the community about Jesus!"

Saduwara fervently cast vision for his village: "Just wait until you return; our *entire* village will be following Jesus!"

"I hope so!" I agreed with excitement. "I believe that is God's vision for this place. We will be praying for that."

We explained baptism to Saduwara. After we assured his understanding of baptism, we asked him, "Do you think you are ready to be baptized?"

"Yes," Saduwara said with joy and confidence, "I am definitely ready."

"Awesome! When we come tomorrow, we will baptize you." We then asked Saduwara an obvious but logistically needed question: "Is there a river nearby?"

Smiling, Saduwara said, "We can go to the river just across this field and down in that valley."

"Okay, we have a plan!" I told him. "Let's pray together and finish our meeting for today." We prayed and were on our way.

Today's the day! I thought as I woke up. *This is going to be so exciting! I can hardly wait to get back to the chief's home and see him baptized.* We packed into our vehicle and headed to Saduwara's house. When we arrived, we did not see the chief waiting for us as usual. We scanned the landscape, but he was nowhere to be seen. Saduwara had several family members who lived nearby, so we walked over to one of their homes.

"Have you seen the chief today?" we inquired. "Do you know where he is?"

"One of the older women is very sick, so he had to take her to the hospital," a village woman answered. "They left early this morning and won't be back until much later. So you won't be able to see him today."

We thanked them and began walking back to our car. On the way, we saw another villager. Gaining more information never hurts, so we asked him, "Do you know when the chief will return?"

"He just went into the nearby town and will be back later," the villager replied.

Hmm, I thought, *that's weird. They are telling two different stories. I wonder if something is going on?*

Testing our uneasy feeling about the situation, we asked a third villager, "Have you seen the chief?"

"He has a government meeting nearby, so he is busy today," he said sternly.

The people's faces were no longer warm and inviting as they had been just a day prior. In fact, the people became suddenly cold and closed off. *Okay, they are definitely lying to us. What is going on?!* I wondered. *Something is off here.* Our small team gathered and prayed against the opposition we began to sense.

Just as we finished praying, the chief's son rolled in and began yelling, "We will not change! We worship the gods in the forest. You will not baptize my father. What you are doing is illegal! Stop teaching my father about Jesus, and never come back! You must leave this place. You are not welcome here."

As Saduwara's son ranted, two Scriptures immediately came to mind. I could see them unfold before our eyes: the first was Matthew 10:35 when Jesus taught that his mission would turn a son against his father; and the second was Mark 4:15–17 which teaches that when the Word of God is scattered like seed, persecution arises and Satan attempts to snatch up the seed, keeping the lost from eternal life!

As soon as Saduwara became serious about Jesus, proclaimed the good news in his village, and stepped forward in obedience for baptism, opposition arose. Saduwara's son began slinging mud and stirred up the entire village to join him. They had become *mudslingers.*

Don't be fooled. Mudrunners attract mudslingers. I find it ironic when I hear stories of soldiers who are absolutely shocked they are being shot at once they hit the battlefield, because they signed up for it! As followers of Jesus it is the same way. We are often shocked when the mud starts flying our way. But we shouldn't be. Jesus, the pioneer mudrunner Himself, said "If the world hates you, keep in mind that it hated me first" (John 15:18 NIV).

It's one thing when the mudslingers are distant acquaintances, strangers, or people far from us. But it's totally another thing (and most often the toughest) when family, friends, and those closest to us start slinging mud. I have faced my share of mudslinging. Joining the race as a mudrunner for Jesus has invited all kinds of mud balls and dirt clods to be hurled my way. Here are just a few of the insults and interrogations that have attempted to muddy my face:

"You are just young and passionate. Every young guy is like you and wants to do these kind of things. Just wait, your passion will die out."

"You are too young to do what you're doing and too young to proclaim these truths."

"The tribe you are focusing on is too small. There are not enough people to strategically invest time there."

"You are not living on ground long-term, so you won't really be able to impact people or make disciples."

"Itinerant ministry is not a valid calling."

"Your strategy is not the right one."

"Is this really what you want to give your life to?"

"Is it really wise to give up all your opportunities for this?"

"Will you really have enough money to live on if you do this?"

"You are a dumb*** kid going overseas. Can you really help those people?"

"Why would you go *there*, when there is so much to be done *here*?"

"You are not with the right agency. You need to quit and join these others, or we will not support you."

"You need to change how you are doing things and do them other ways."

"Change your message or you're done."

"There is no way God would call you to those places. It is too dangerous. You are not wise to go there."

"I never saw you as someone who could do these kinds of things."

"What education do you have to be able to do what you are doing? Is it really enough?"

The mudslinging naysayers have been many. While some have been non-Christians (as in the story of Saduwara and his son), I am sad to say that most of these words have come from fellow brothers and sisters in Christ and, at times, people close to me. While some have been well-meaning, many have missed the heart and mission of Jesus with their words.

At times, I've become so caked in mud, all I can do is scrape it off by prayerfully recalling God's truth, calling, and promises. Have you faced mudslingers? If not yet, as a mudrunner you will. And when you do, allow the water of God's Word to cleanse you and wash away the mud. Shoes caked in mud become heavier and heavier. Unwashed mud from mudslingers will slowly weigh you down, discourage you, and tempt you to quit the race altogether. Don't let it. Perhaps these truths God has provided me in moments of facing mudslinging will encourage and help you scrape off some of the mud:

We must not let anyone look down upon us if we are young, but rather set an example for all the believers!

God can use the young to radically reach the world and often has throughout history!

God cares about the few! Even just one person is enough to go for, just like the parable of the shepherd leaving the ninety-nine sheep for one!

God has used itinerant ministry (traveling from place to place) throughout the Scriptures, in the life of Jesus Himself, and throughout history for mighty kingdom impact!

When it comes to God's kingdom cause, we each need strategies uniquely birthed by the Holy Spirit. And rather than throwing stones at each other's unique styles, methods, and callings, we must link arms for the sake of His kingdom!

If Jesus has said, "Go!" we must continue going, no matter how foolish it looks and no matter what we are required to give up for His sake!

Obedience to Jesus is the only qualification we really need.

The truth is, you are not alone in this. Many who have stepped out to run the race have faced the naysaying mudslingers. And who really cares what they say anyway? You are not living for the approval of anyone but Jesus our King. And Jesus Himself was abandoned, backstabbed, betrayed, mocked, and spit on—all before His flogging and crucifixion. In fact, even Jesus' own beloved disciples discouraged Him to fulfill His purpose on the cross, failed to support Him in prayer during one of the heaviest moments of His life, and even denied that they knew Him.

God often advances His kingdom through opposition. Movement only occurs through friction; just think about the rubber tires of a car gripping the pavement to move forward. It seems the same is true spiritually as well. The early Church leader and apologist Tertullian declared, "The blood of the martyrs is the seed of the church." If you engage with godly conviction and humility when the mud starts flying, you will experience supercharged spiritual growth, joy, and blessing. The more the friction, the more you will move forward. In God's kingdom, rewards are found in opposition, difficulty, and suffering.

So, keep going! Enduring opposition at the hands of mudslingers is worth it because Jesus is worthy of it. Do not give up! Do not grow weary in doing good, "for in due season we will reap, if we do not give up" (Galatians 6:9 ESV).

Now What?

- Have you faced any mudslinging naysayers who have come against God's desire for your life? When it comes to the mud that may be launched at you, what are you most afraid of?
- Pray and tell the Lord that you give Him your fear. Ask

Him to expel your fear by His love. If anyone has already hurt you by slinging mud, forgive them in prayer now: *Lord, I forgive this mudslinger for what they did.*

- What is a truth that God may want you to hold onto going forward?

SIXTEEN

UNQUALIFIED

WE AWOKE to the sound of children playing. Their giggling and occasional high-pitched bantering was accompanied by the elevated, abrupt click language of the adults exchanging morning conversation. Nathan and I unzipped our tent, stepped out, and started a fire to make breakfast. Our campsite menu consisted of a few biscuits, leftover rice from the night before, and some instant coffee.

With breakfast behind us, we gathered our discipleship materials. Among them were our Bibles, Hadza audio Bible players, and Bible story pictures. Supplies in hand, we began the fifteen-minute walk to Kiula's hut.

As we approached Kiula's hut, we yelled out the morning greeting, "Shyahmo mutana!" Expecting a greeting in return, we heard none. That seemed odd to us. So we began scanning the area surrounding his hut. Perhaps Kiula and his wife had already started their workday. Still no sight of either of them.

We stood at the doorway of Kiula's hut and peered inside. Things were motionless; both Kiula and his wife were nowhere to be found. A bit confused, we journeyed back to the main village area and began to ask around, "Have you seen Kiula or his wife?"

After a few shoulder shrugs and a smattering of people saying "I don't know," someone finally answered, "I think they went drinking somewhere."

"Where would that be?" we inquired.

With her finger pointed toward the bush, she answered in a way that allowed us to fill in the blanks. "The Datoga tribe makes the local alcohol," she said.

We began walking in the direction she pointed. We asked another tribal member where we might find local alcohol. Again, like a needle on a compass, the man pointed his finger. The correct direction validated, we continued.

Another kilometer ahead, our suspicions were confirmed. We saw Kiula lying face down in the dirt, a 1.5-liter water bottle strapped on his back. I grabbed the bottle, opened it, and sniffed. Clearly, it wasn't water! Whew! We surely got a good whiff of strong local moonshine. I poured the moonshine into the dirt as we tried to wake Kiula.

"Kiula," we said. But he lay there motionless.

We addressed him a little louder. "Kiula, Kiula." Still nothing.

The third time we yelled and jostled his arm. "Kiula! Wake up!"

Kiula opened his eyes, squinting at the brightness of the day. We helped him to his feet. He could hardly stand, let alone walk. Snot was drizzling from his nose as if he had just been pepper sprayed. It was not a good sight.

I felt quite discouraged by Kiula's decision. He was one of the key people we had chosen to teach Bible stories so that he could share them with others. We were intending to train him as a disciple maker. His indulgences were putting all those plans in jeopardy.

Taking a deep breath, I was reminded that Christians are people who live by grace. *Let's try again tomorrow,* I thought. *Everyone makes mistakes sometimes.*

Evening came and went. The next morning brought a new day but the same unfortunate story with Kiula. We found Kiula and his wife in the same place as the previous day. Bottles of moon-shine from nearby Datoga huts lay empty beside them; once again, they were passed-out drunk.

This is one of our so-called disciples, I thought. *How in the world are we going to continue teaching him Bible stories day by day if this is how he is living?*

Kiula repeated his drunken behavior for days. Making the situation worse, some others we were spiritually investing in decided to join Kiula and his wife in the "fun." Their drinking binge wasn't a one-off. It wasn't a one-day regrettable indiscretion of poor judgment. No, they willfully chose what they wanted day after day after day. They were passed-out, flat-on-their-faces, can't-stand-up drunk for five days straight. I had never seen people as inebriated as they seemed to be able to get themselves. Their choices were harmful to them and damaging to the mission. They also brought great discouragement to our team.

Teaching anyone anything while they're in a drunken state isn't the best strategy. And teaching anyone who is passed out drunk is no better than speaking to a wall. Spiritually investing in these new disciples just wasn't going to happen this week. So, we did the only thing we could do. We waited for their drunken stupor to come to an end. Our idle time gave ample space for questions and doubts to fill my mind: *Lord, have we wasted our time? Is all our effort pointless? Has our work amounted to anything? God, how will You even cause disciples to be made here? Where is the faith? Is this even possible? Should we pack our bags, give up, and go home? Are we even qualified to deal with this?*

To me the mission felt impossible. I was losing hope. I felt like a failure. Have you ever felt discouraged when things weren't going in the direction you thought God was taking them? Or disheartened when your discipleship efforts seem miniscule and unimportant? I surely have—and more often than I wish or care to admit. Discipleship can often seem dark and impossible, especially if we get into the nitty-gritty mud puddles of human need.

I have experienced this reality both around the globe and at home: I have spent precious time investing in others only for them to disregard and turn their backs on the truth, saying things like the following:

> "I do not believe in Jesus anymore. I am now an atheist."
>
> "Could you please stop using *Jesus* when you pray? I prefer to stick with the generic term *God* now, because we can't limit 'god' to one being."
>
> "I know God has made me this way, but I prefer to be another gender."
>
> "I no longer believe in the validity of Christianity. I mean, clearly the Scriptures are not trustworthy. They were written and developed just like all other religions of the world."

No one enjoys pouring out their heart and investing great amounts of time and energy with someone only to see them walk away and throw it all away. It's disheartening, frustrating, confusing, even maddening and angering. And it makes it easy to want to throw your hands in the air and just give up. It is easy to let discouragement take over when your "disciples" take wrong turns. At times it can make you feel like a failure—as if you don't really have what it takes, as if you are unqualified for this mission.

As we waited for our Hadzabe "disciples" to recover from their drunken binge, God spoke to me and cut to my heart as I read these sobering verses:

> *Brothers and sisters, think of what you were when you were called. Not many of you were wise by human standards; not many were influential; not many were of noble birth. But God chose the foolish things of the world to shame the wise; God chose the weak things of the world to shame the strong. God chose the lowly things of this world and the despised things—and the things that are not—to nullify the things that are, so that no one may boast before him (1 Corinthians 1:26–29 NIV).*

As I read, God began teaching me and reminding me of the truth. Yes, some of the disciples we were working with did seem "weak," "lowly," and "despised." Yet God seemed to be choosing them. It was as if God wanted to prove to the world what He alone is capable of—choosing, transforming, and using those who are unwanted, unfinished, underwhelming, and unqualified!

And the message became even more personal. It was not only about those I was investing in but also about me. Time and again, God chooses and uses the lowly and despised, the nothings of this world—so that no one can boast! With little to none to boast about, I was included among the unqualified God could use for His glory.

As we run this race, the finish line may feel far with no end in sight. More mud, more mud, more mud around every corner. Many of us may feel like our spiritual investments come to absolutely nothing, further fueling our inadequacies of feeling unqualified! If that is you, then you are in good company. Peter and John, Jesus' disciples and well-known followers, were "unschooled, ordinary men," yet all the people were amazed by their courage (Acts 4:13 NIV). How could they speak such words? And with such courage? The people "took note that these men had been with Jesus" (Acts 4:13 NIV). Peter and John knew what truly counts: being with Jesus! Have you been up close with Jesus? Then you have what it takes—even if you are "unqualified" in the eyes of others.

People have often asked me, "What are your qualifications?"

Whenever I hear this question, all I can think of is Philippians 3:8–10 where Paul the apostle considers all of his accomplishments as "garbage" in comparison with knowing Jesus Christ his Lord. While our soft, "Sunday-morning friendly" English translations use the word "garbage," Paul actually uses a much stronger word in the original Greek writing. Paul considers his "grand" human achievements total "crap" compared to what God can accomplish in and through him.

So what are my qualifications? I have begun to say that my only qualifications are Jesus Himself and His calling for my life.

Everything else really doesn't matter that much. Jesus is our first, highest, and most essential qualification!

Yet so many people continue to feel inadequate for the mission. It could be that you are diminishing how God has uniquely made you and disqualify yourself before even getting started, all based on someone else's measuring stick and standard.

Maybe you have fallen prey to such thinking. Maybe you feel unqualified because you don't think you know enough about the Bible or don't have the "proper" education. Perhaps you feel unqualified due to present struggles, thinking, *Oh man, I just messed up again!* or *I cannot believe I am still struggling with this sin in my life! Will I ever get over this?* Maybe you can't get past your history. "You have no idea about my past life," you might say. "You don't know what I have done. I can't be qualified; I'm damaged goods."

If that is you, I have one thought for you: banana bread. I know I might sound crazy right now, but just go with my crazy brain for a second. I always remember being so excited when my mom would take warm banana bread filled with melting chocolate chips out of the oven. So delicious! Now where did this amazing bread come from? My mom made this delicious bread from nasty, brown, beaten, battered, and bruised bananas that began leaking juice because they had been left out on the counter far too long. Just when these bananas could have been easily thrown out, they still had a purpose.

You may feel bruised, battered, and beat up by the struggles of life. But God still has a purpose for you! This is what Jesus meant when He shared the truth that those who are forgiven much, love much (Luke 7:47). To be forgiven of a lot means you have sinned a whole lot. And Jesus is saying, He still has a purpose for you. You will be able to connect with others in their struggles and reveal the love of God in a powerful and practical way because you have been where they are.

If you're stuck in a struggle, confess your sin to Jesus and press forward. Do not dwell on your sin and how awful it is; rather, live in the reality of what Jesus paid for on the cross. You are not "unqualified" based on the judgment of others and their inability to get past what Jesus has already forgiven. So, if someone says you can't make an impact based on your past, kindly disregard their faulty theology!

I also wonder how many of us disqualify ourselves due to fear. We wonder what will happen or what won't happen, so we don't act. We allow fear to have the final say and paralyze us as doubt creeps in. We wonder why Jesus feels so far away when He claims to be near.

Jesus said, "Go and make disciples of all nations . . . And surely I am with you *always*" (Matthew 28: 19–20 NIV, italics mine). In spite of our fear, we must step out in faith. And as we do, we experience the radical reality of Jesus *with* us! Do you wonder why His presence seems to be lacking and fear seems to be filling every crevice? Maybe it's time to simply step out in obedience and trust that His "perfect love casts out fear" (1 John 4:18 ESV).

Your past and present struggles don't disqualify you. Neither does your education. Neither do you need to let your fear level disqualify you, nor even . . . your age!

I remember doing a disciple-making training in South Asia when a young man stood up and said, "God is leading me to go and share the good news in [unspecified region]. There are very few believers there and the Hindus strongly persecute Christians. The gospel is needed there, but I am only seventeen years old! What should I do?"

My younger brother in Christ was essentially saying, "Do I have what it takes? Am I too young? Am I really qualified for this?"

I knew the feeling all too well, so I told him, "You can do this, brother! You have been with Jesus, and that is what truly matters. He will be with you as you go. And you can set an example for all the believers. Many scholars think Jeremiah the prophet was only seventeen years old when God first called and sent him to go. Many even think that some of the disciples might have begun as teenagers. I am excited to hear about how Jesus uses you!"

Don't allow others to disqualify you from what God is up to.

Not strangers. Not enemies. Not well-intended but stuck-up believers. Not even your closest family and friends. That's above your pay grade. Let God alone determine how qualified you are for His plans and mission.

I remember talking with my great-uncle Trevor about the "unqualified," and he shared this story with me, declaring it as one of his most exciting moments on the mission field:

"There was an Indian guy who was not allowed to preach in the local church assembly because he did not have enough education. So I decided to take him to the tribal people and said, 'Why don't you preach here?' God began using this 'uneducated' brother to bring countless people to Jesus. Now, years later, they have made him a leader with the mission organization, Indian Evangelical Mission. Charlie, never overlook those who are undervalued by others!"

As you advance God's kingdom cause and lunge into the mud puddles of human need, you may appear "unqualified" by the world's standards. When "disqualifiers" take a run at you, simply run to Jesus! He really is the only qualifier and qualification we need.

As you run with Jesus, don't lose sight of what it feels like to be "unqualified" as one of His chosen vessels. You will likely encounter others who are feeling the same—lowly and despised, overlooked and discounted by many. Pay attention! They may very well be God's first choice for the mission ahead.

Now What?

- What has caused you to feel unqualified to make an impact for God's kingdom? Are there any specific struggles, fears, statements made by "disqualifiers," or something else that hinders you?
- What do you believe God wants you to do, despite your lack of "qualification" in the world's eyes? And as a result, what does God want you to do right now with whatever is making you feel "unqualified"?

- Who in your life might be undervalued and overlooked by others? How could you come alongside them in their lives, encourage ("breathe courage into") them, and empower them in the Lord?

SEVENTEEN

OUR RUNNING COMPANION

THE JOURNEY WAS AGONIZING. We faced several break-downs. We were stranded in the middle of nowhere. We slept on wooden benches in random local schools. And then there was our vehicle. It moved at a snail's pace—five miles per hour, to be exact —unless one of us hopped out with a wrench and tapped on the engine's fuel intake while the other pumped the gas pedal. That mechanical wizardry thrust our car to fifteen miles per hour for a grand total of three minutes! Looking back, I'm not sure why we didn't pronounce the car dead on the side of the road and give it a proper burial!

God had been leading me and Nathan to another region to pioneer more Hadzabe villages. After overcoming many obstacles and hazards like the ones above, we finally arrived on the other side of Lake Eyasi (the central salt lake around which all Hadzabe live). We parked our failure-of-a-car at a village school and found a man willing to drive us the rest of the way to our intended destination . . . as always, "for a small price."

When we arrived in the bush town, we met a young man who promised to show us the way to the Hadzabe village. We accepted his offer, and he crammed into the car with us.

Not long into our journey, we rolled up to a river crossing. Our driver stopped, looked at the water, and said to us, "Now is your time to get out."

Given the questionable depth of the water and the size of the car, we agreed that exiting seemed like the best option. We hopped out of the car and dropped all our gear on the ground. And off our driver went . . . only, not across the river, but back the other direction! Hiking would be our only option from that point on.

We picked up our backpacks and began the trek, the afternoon sun scorching our face and neck. The unanticipated hike was draining. The only relief came in taking brief respites as we shared greetings with the people living in huts along the way. When we reached the far end of the village, we met a local named Musa. His greeting was kind and refreshing. "My name is Musa," he said. "Welcome to our village! We are happy to have you stay on our land."

Shortly after, several women welcomed us and said, "Give us your clothes. They need to be washed. And you need to take a shower. We will send some young men to bring buckets of water from the river bed."

You know you smell raunchy when the local bush-people tell you it's time to take a shower! It had only been a week since we last showered. That's not an unusually long time between showers when out in the bush. Yet apparently our sweaty stench caused the locals to feel otherwise! We were delighted for the opportunity to clean up. There was only one problem: we had no other clothes except for the ones on our backs!

Half laughing and slightly uncomfortable, I looked at Nathan and asked, "What on Earth are we going to do if they want to take our clothes to wash them?!"

"I know!" Nathan said, talking and giggling simultaneously. "This is going to be so awkward!"

We put on our strategic thinking caps and concluded: when in the bush, do as the bushmen do! So, we wrapped ourselves in our small bed blankets. Problem solved! After a good scrubbing and the return of freshly laundered clothes, we got dressed and went to interact with more of the villagers.

While we had many meaningful conversations that evening, one encounter was particularly meaningful. It was with a young man named Enjilay. Nathan and I enjoyed conversing with Enjilay, and our conversation about everyday things led effortlessly to sharing the message of the gospel. And Enjilay said yes to Jesus for the first time in his life! Our conversations with Enjilay only increased as we spent time in his village. Enjilay would often stick around long after others had left, and we would find a log or rock to sit on and talk about life, Jesus, or anything else on our minds.

One day Enjilay revealed the burden of his heart as he shared the meaning of his name with us. "My older brother died, and my parents decided to name me Enjilay," he said. Then, pausing as if it was too painful to say, he gutted out, "Enjilay means 'replacement.' I really hate it!"

Enjilay looked at us with a certain amount of hope in his eyes that wanted to believe that what he was about to ask could actually be granted. Then he asked, "Can I have a new name?"

"Actually, yes, yes you can!" I answered. "God often gave new names to many of His followers. We think you should pray and ask God to reveal a new name to you."

We had no idea what might actually happen, but we were confident that the living Jesus would actively engage Enjilay. We believed in the nearness of our God who personally teaches and equips us (Psalm 119:102; Hebrews 13:20–21), and we trusted He would meet Enjilay in the midst of his struggles.

A few days later, Enjilay came to us and said, "Last night while everyone was sleeping, I heard a voice calling out to me. It said, 'Ezekieli, Ezekieli, Ezekieli.'"

We rejoiced with him. "God has renamed you Ezekiel!"

No longer a "replacement," Ezekieli was so excited about the living God he had just encountered that he could not keep it to Himself. Ezekieli began rounding up others to hear the Bible stories we were sharing each day!

His excitement to tell God's story kept expanding. "There are some Hadzabe in nearby villages who are unreached," he shared. "Can we go there and teach them too?"

"Ezekieli, why don't you go teach them when we leave?" I urged him. "In the same way Jesus is with *us* as we go, He is also with *you* as you go!"

Jesus not only went with Enjilay; He also goes with you. Jesus is not simply the one we run for; He's actually the one we run *with*. Jesus is our running companion!

That said, I fear that far too often we're tempted to run the race on our own. We live, serve, and run as if Jesus is still dead rather than alive and active today. We share ideas and talk *about* God without really engaging Him. We ignore His presence when all the while He is right in the middle of whatever we're doing, wherever we are. We feel the pressure to come up with answers for others and provide them solutions for what only Jesus can provide. We mutter passionless prayers at gatherings, bedtimes, and before meals—all the while, practically ignoring our closest Companion and Friend we're praying to.

We have done plenty *for* God. It is time for us to link arms with the resurrected Jesus and run this race *with* Him! Just as an arrow cannot fly far without a bow, neither will you be able to run well without engaging Jesus who is altogether present and with you.

Have you been living and ministering *with* Jesus or only *for* Him? Maybe you need to take some extended time alone with Jesus and see what He has to say (Luke 10:38–42). Perhaps you need to acknowledge His presence throughout your busy day. When issues arise and decisions need to be made, maybe you need to pause to pray and listen for His guidance before you come up with a solution or make a choice. Whatever you do, do it *with* Jesus!

You have an all-powerful, active running companion who is with you always. As with Enjilay, God does not see you as a "replacement" but as a one-of-a-kind creation worth sharing His life with. As you lace up your running shoes, don't forget God is waiting for you to run the race *with* Him. Knowing that God is running with us changes our perspective of every hurdle, decision, and leg of the race we face.

Now What?

- Have you been living like Jesus is dead and simply doing things *for* Him? Or have you been living as if Jesus is alive, doing life *with* Him as with a best friend? What has this looked like in your life?
- Knowing that Jesus is alive, active, and present in the race with us, how does this change your perspective?
- How can you intentionally acknowledge and engage the near presence of Jesus throughout your days this week?

EIGHTEEN

FAITH FILLED

"YOU HAVE COME ALL this way, my friend. Did you bring me a gift?" Amisi quizzically inquired.

Amisi was one of the many neighboring locals we met near Mary's home. He was forty-something, skinny, with short hair, a thin mustache, and a face not easily forgotten. He smoked often and carried a consistent cough that proved it. Amisi was a kind man, approachable, and always willing to sit and talk with us whenever we were around.

When we arrived at Mary's home after a long journey, Amisi came by to greet us. He was on Mary's doorstep no sooner than we could step out of the Land Cruiser. That's when Amisi asked me about a gift.

Unfortunately, I hadn't planned to bring a gift for Amisi. So, I jokingly turned the tables. "I have traveled all this way to come and see you. Did you bring *me* a gift?!" I inquired.

Amisi laughed. His hopes weren't high on receiving anything. I'm sure he thought it was at least worth a try. Later, I pulled a lighter from my gear and gave it to Amisi. Firestarter is always a good gift for bush people, and being generous and kind goes a long way in the kingdom life. When Amisi saw the gift, he lit up

(pun intended). Humor and laughter, by the way, are also benefi-
cial in life and ministry.

Somewhere amid a lull in our visit, Amisi asked, "Do you
remember the woman I took you to pray for last year?" Honestly, I
did not. As Amisi began filling in the details, however, the
memory began falling into place for me . . .

One year earlier, we had been at Mary's home, and Amisi came
by. Knowing we were people of God, he asked, "Will you come
with me to pray for a woman who is sick?" We agreed and
followed Amisi, not knowing where we were going or what to
expect. After walking a mile or so from Mary's place, we arrived at
the woman's home. We stepped inside the small mud-brick house.
Some family were present to help attend to the woman who was
lying in her bed on the opposite side of the room. We politely
nodded to the others, but our eyes were immediately drawn to the
woman's legs. They were thick and swollen, the size of tree trunks.
She couldn't walk. It was not a good sight; something was severely
wrong.

As the woman sat up, we greeted each other in the Hadzabe
tribal click language.

"Mutana," she uttered.

"Mutana," we replied.

She did not understand English, and we only knew a few
Hadzabe words. But we knew just enough of the trade language,
Kiswahili, to get around. So, we did our best to exchange basic
conversation with the woman and her family members. Having no
translator present and lacking the needed language skills to
communicate well, our connection was awkward and brief.

It became clear that the best way to proceed was to talk with
the one who not only knows and hears all languages, but speaks
them as well—Jesus. We anointed the woman's head with oil, laid
our hands on her, and prayed, "Lord, will you heal this woman, in
Jesus' name? Jesus, will you reveal Yourself in this place? Your
kingdom come and will be done! Amen."

After we finished praying, we gave the woman the only thing
we knew to offer her in addition to our prayers: an audio player

with Bible stories that had been recorded in her Hadzabe language. We said our good-byes and made our way back to Mary's house.

We had no idea what might happen. Yet, we trusted Jesus. We knew Jesus was able to heal her, and even more, we knew He could take hold of her life and grip her heart.

Back at Mary's home one year later, our conversation with Amisi brought our hearts great excitement. "You know that woman with the swollen legs," Amisi continued, "the one you guys came and prayed for? Well, she is now walking without any trouble. She has been healed! And get this, she listens to that Hadzabe audio Bible every day."

We offered a simple-faith prayer one year earlier, and God did the miraculous as a testimony and witness for the gospel! Although I had believed Jesus could heal (and had seen the Lord miraculously heal others before), I was shocked that Jesus used us in such a way. We were full of joy knowing that Jesus broke through into that woman's home . . . His kingdom come indeed!

I love how Hebrews 11 describes the faith-filled life: "Now faith is the assurance of things hoped for, the conviction of things not seen. . . . By faith Abraham . . . went out, not knowing where he was going. . . . By faith Sarah herself received power to conceive, even when she was past the age . . . . By faith the people crossed the Red Sea as on dry land . . . By faith the walls of Jericho fell down" (Hebrews 11:1, 8, 11, 29, 30 ESV).

Faith is not only how we begin our life with Jesus (Ephesians 2:8), but it is how we live life with Jesus day by day (1 Corinthians 16:13). We continually trust Him, look to Him, and expect Him to do what is currently unseen. He is the one who "calls into existence the things that do not exist" (Romans 4:17 ESV).

Are you facing a situation that is waiting for God's kingdom to break through? What if you began to look at your situation through the eyes of faith, dreaming about what God could do, can do, and might desire to do? What if you prayed with simple faith, *Your kingdom come, Jesus, and your will be done*? God just might begin to call into being—both in you and through you—that which has not yet been.

It has commonly been said, "Faith is spelled R-I-S-K." To live by faith is a call to risk. Abraham had to leave his hometown without knowing what would happen. Sarah had to trust that God would do the impossible no matter what others thought. The Israelites had to believe that God would continue to hold the waters at bay. Joshua had to follow an out-of-the-box battle plan! God may ask you to leave behind your comfort, believe the impossible, step into the unknown, and do something that makes absolutely no sense. To live a faith-filled life, you must be willing to risk!

Risking isn't complicated. It necessitates, however, a courage built on trust. Living by faith each day requires absolute trust in our sovereign God. And as you courageously trust Him, you will begin to witness God do far more than you could ask or imagine (Ephesians 3:20).

Risk is worth it. Whether praying for a stranger and trusting God to break through or buying a one-way plane ticket to an unknown country, God is worth trusting and believing. He brings "the assurance of things hoped for" and provides us with "conviction of things not seen." The glorious adventure of a faith-filled life is well worth it, for Jesus is worthy of it!

Now What?

- When was a time you stepped out in faith, not knowing what God was going to do?
- The adventure of a faith-filled life requires risk. What are you afraid of risking?
- How is God calling you to step out in faith during this season of life? Ask Him right now, *Lord, what does the faith-filled life look like for me?*

NINETEEN

FAITH FORWARD

SOME OF THE most amazing moments of life happen when we step out in faith and see God's kingdom break through. That said, what happens when we are still awaiting a miracle, conception hasn't occurred, we don't see the sea splitting, the walls haven't fallen, and the battle still rages? How strong is our faith in the unseen, unknown, and not-yet-won moments?

I remember meeting a little boy named Harry. He would always come by our camp and whisper something I could hardly hear. At first, I wondered if he was even speaking or simply mouthing a word. I would motion for him to speak louder, and he would raise his voice maybe a millionth of a decibel. The volume increase didn't help; I still couldn't catch it.

Again and again I would ask him to speak louder as I put my ear near his mouth. Then, finally, I caught it. He said, "Ndizi." Harry was asking for a ndizi, the Swahili word for banana. I gladly gave this little boy a banana. I'd do just about anything to put a smile on his face. Why? Because Harry had alcoholic parents who would often beat him and his siblings. These kids were left hungry with nothing to eat day after day. Some nights, we would be awakened by agonizing screams. It was coming from their home nearly a half mile up the hill from our tent! Yes, giving Harry a banana was the least I could do for him. Truthfully, I never really knew what else to do. Harry's situation felt hopeless.

Harry's life is just one of many situations that have felt disheartening. On another occasion, we were sitting around our camp and a young Hadza man named Nayehnay walked by. We invited him to sit down. Nayehnay began telling us what was happening in his village area. His words were filled with hurt and pain.

"Wealthy foreigners purchased land from the government and set up a game camp. Tourists come to sleep and hunt there. Because they don't want to lose potential profit, this tourist hunting business does not want us hunting in the region. But hunting is our way of life and livelihood. It is how we survive!"

"Wow. That is so difficult," I said. "So, how are you all handling this situation?"

"Some of us secretly hunt," Nayehnay answered. "We go by night and return early in the morning so we can hide the animals we bring back. But one time, I hunted a large water buffalo in the middle of the day. I looked around to make sure no one was watching. When I returned to the village, I found a group of 'military men' waiting for me. Somehow they saw me; I hear they take pictures from the sky." *Most likely a drone*, I thought.

Nayehnay continued, "These men surrounded me and beat me relentlessly. I managed to jump out of their circle and run away. I ran up the mountain near the village. Two of the men chased me while the others stayed in the village to keep watch.

"I eluded the two men on the mountain and cautiously maneuvered my way back to the village to get my belongings. I had barely been able to grab my shoes and shirt when they spotted me. They pulled out their weapons and started shooting. I didn't even have the chance to grab my bow and arrows. Bullets whizzed by me as I ran off. I just kept running and running and running. All night long I ran.

"Finally, I made it to a village in a neighboring region. I lived in hiding there for two years. I couldn't return home because those soldiers were constantly scouring the region looking for me."

We listened intently to Nayehnay. His story stirred us, as compassion as well as shock and anger filled our hearts.

"You know, I am not the only one with these troubles," Nayehnay said. "Many are having problems because of this foreign tourist company. They do not like Hadzabe people hunting near their land. If they get word that anyone has been hunting, they send men to our village to investigate who it is. These men intimidate and beat people until someone breaks and shares the name of the hunter. Then they track down the hunter and beat him. If the hunter doesn't die from his beating, they drum up charges and have him thrown in prison."

We wondered what could be done. "Why doesn't someone go tell the government what is happening and seek help?" we asked.

A sense of hopelessness in his eyes, Nayehnay replied, "We have tried. Everyone who has gone to the local government to complain about this injustice and to seek hunting rights has ended up dead."

I fumed with righteous anger the rest of the day. Apparently, a foreign company can come in, pay the government, take land, and force those who live on the land to leave. What injustice! I thought, *Let's grab the guns and go take care of this ourselves!* As I was praying later that day, I shared with God that I could really relate to the psalmist as he prayed for judgment upon his enemies (Psalm 54:5; Psalm 3:7; Psalm 109:6–15). My prayer became, *Lord, I will do whatever it takes to see your justice come here!*

As I prayed, however, God cautioned me, *"Who are you to take that place?"* God reminded me that He is the one who takes vengeance; it's our job to forgive as well as bless our enemies (Romans 12:19–20). God's Word moved my heart, compelling me to pray, *Lord, I choose to forgive these people. Have your way. You are the judge; I am not.*

The entire situation looked hopeless from my vantage point. I could not see any positive changes on the horizon. Yet, I trusted that God would somehow make all things right.

Romans 4:17 (NIV) proclaims the encouraging reality that God "calls into being things that were not," including the promise to make Abraham a father of many nations. But Romans 4:18 (NIV) reveals that it was not all easy for Abraham: "Against all hope, Abraham in hope believed." Abraham couldn't see what God saw on the horizon. He had no idea how the changes God promised could even take place. Even still, Abraham believed and trusted that God would make a way and fulfill His promise.

Hebrews 11 is packed full of breakthrough moments realized by faith-filled followers. But it is also packed full of those who lived with faith-forward trust. They did not yet see the promise fulfilled. They did not yet taste the fullness of victory. Still, they held onto faith for the future: "All these, though commended through their faith, did not receive what was promised, since God had provided something better" (Hebrews 11:39–40 ESV). They awaited the coming Jesus.

The same may be true in our lives. We may not see the breakthrough just yet. So we wait, and we live with faith-forward trust, longing for Jesus to return and make all things right.

Although we cannot see it now, we can be sure that when Jesus comes again, He will fully restore all of creation! When Jesus comes, He will hold accountable those who were responsible for the injustice among the Hadzabe. This includes Nayehnay's abusers. They will face God's judgment. And little Harry's parents too. They also will be held accountable. Justice will be served. In fact, God will make all things right for all who have been wronged —whoever they are, wherever they live, whatever the circumstances.

And on the great day of the Lord's return, Hadzabe believers— together with all believers worldwide—will be overwhelmed with great joy in the presence of Jesus as they realize that all they had hoped for and longed for has come to completion.

As believers we have certain hope in Christ's coming kingdom, where all injustice will be righted, all hunger eliminated, all sickness healed, all tears wiped away, and all wars terminated. And on that day, the very best of all—we will see Jesus face-to-face and fully experience the very presence of God!

Where are you these days? Are you stuck between the promise and the breakthrough? You may not know where you are going. You may not know what's around the corner. You may not know how light will pierce the darkness in your situation. But will you trust the One—Jesus—who does know?

Those in the Bible who lived faith-forward lives didn't know the process or the details or the means of getting there—but they trusted God would bring about the ultimate promised outcome. In their present, they did not even receive the fullness of what was promised. In the end, they received all God promised and more because they, in faith, believed and trusted Him all along the way.

Maybe you are clinging to promises currently unfulfilled. Maybe you see no outcome on your horizon. Trust God. Seek Him. Maybe Jesus will break through for you, as He did with healing power for the Hadzabe woman who couldn't walk, as He did for Abraham and Sarah, and as He has done for countless others. Or maybe you will have to wait with groaning and longing until He comes again to set all creation free from bondage to decay and corruption (Romans 8:18–25). Although our sightline is often limited to what is right in front of us, we must not lose sight of the true finish line, where Jesus will greet us with a "Well done, good and faithful servant!" (Matthew 25:23 ESV).

You may not see how the journey, the paths, or the plans will take you to the end. But by faith, you can be (and are) assured of the final outcome. Jesus promised it, and so with certainty we know it is true—He's coming again! And on that day, all things will be completed and fulfilled in Him. All darkness will be destroyed. He will make all things right. The race will be won!

Now What?

- Have you faced or are you currently facing a situation in which the miracle, breakthrough, or victory has not yet been seen? What does this look like?

- Is there an injustice you have faced or seen in the
  world that has infuriated you? Have you been able to
  forgive others, hand your situation over to God, and
  trust Him as the ultimate judge (for vengeance is His)?
- How does it encourage you knowing that Jesus is
  coming again to make all things right? How can you
  keep this in the forefront of your mind when tragedy
  strikes?

TWENTY

CHASING WANDERERS

I SQUEEZED onto a motorcycle with my two friends, Omar and Prim, and we ventured into the rainy night to find the local red-light district. Although brothels and street prostitution are quite open in some areas of South Asia, they aren't in this country. So we had to do some investigating to discover where these hidden (and illegal) activities were taking place. My white American appearance wouldn't be advantageous to our search. The black rain jacket, green baseball cap, and dark riding mask I was wearing helped resolve that issue. We parked the motorcycle outside a dimly lit hotel area and began to look around.

We took note of a building with lit candles in the window next to the entrance. Omar said what all three of us were thinking: "Guys, this might be the place!"

We approached the building to discover if it was the kind of establishment we were looking for. We needed a place we could sit down while searching out potential inroads for any shady, under-the-table business that might be going on.

"Do you sell alcohol here?" Omar asked someone near the entrance. The answer would be helpful in knowing if we were on the right track.

"No," was the reply.

Seeing a family seated at a table just inside the front door along with the "no alcohol" news indicated to us we needed to take our search elsewhere.

Walking a bit further down the narrow street, we came to a hotel. Prim recognized the owner. We greeted him and briefly chatted. Then Prim discreetly let the owner in on what we were doing.

"We are trying to find out where prostitution is happening," Prim said softly. "We want to help them escape that lifestyle."

The owner motioned for us to follow him inside. He closed the door and sat us down at a table in the lobby.

"You guys are doing a good thing," he said. "You know, prostitution and sex trafficking are rampant in this area. Some of the hotel owners are allowing it to happen at their hotels. You may want to talk to the rickshaw drivers [a *rickshaw* is a three-wheeled bicycle that has a bench seat on the back and taxis people around]. Most of those drivers know where to take you if you ask. But be careful in setting up a meeting with some of the girls, because the police occasionally do raids."

We thanked the owner for his help and went to find some rickshaw drivers. Finding them was easy; getting them to give us helpful information was another story. Not sure what our next move should be, we returned to Prim's home for the night. We were done for the evening, but our search wasn't over. We trusted that the Lord who had led us this far would not leave us hanging.

The next day, we continued our search. We drove to another area of the city, and God's plan began to unfold in unexpected ways. Traveling down a side street, we brought our motorcycle to a stop. Incredibly, on the motorcycle stopped just ahead of us was a man named Radhesh, who we had met just several days before. Though Radhesh had shared his heart for those trafficked and abused, we had never made any further plans with him.

Omar told him what we were doing, and Radhesh said, "Let me see what I can do. I think I might be able to find an agent [otherwise known as a pimp] for us to interact with." It seemed that God had provided us a divine appointment!

Later, Radhesh called to share the news. "I have contacted some people and set up an opportunity for you to connect with the agents. The opportunity looks promising."

That night, Omar and another friend named Aarush went to meet the agents, and they setup a time to spend with two girls. Omar and Aarush picked up the girls with a taxi and began the journey to a hotel. The girls had no idea what was happening nor who the two men taking them were. They just expected to service another customer. While Omar and Aarush told the girls that they were bringing them to a meeting with some foreigners, they had not yet shared any details.

Later on, one of the girls revealed that she had been very anxious at this point and was thinking, *I don't know very much English. I hope this goes okay. I have never been with a foreign customer before.*

Omar and Aarush arranged a hotel room and a meal for the two girls. The men then explained that some people were coming to bless them, spend time together, and simply learn about their lives.

Later that evening, the rest of us arrived for the secret meeting. My wife, Dara, and I joined Omar in a hotel meeting room with one of the girls, while another couple joined Prim and the other girl in a rented hotel room. It was late, and no one apart from hotel staff was around.

Dara and I entered the room, sat down, took a deep breath, and smiled at the girl sitting across from us.

"Hi, my name is Dara," my wife began.

"And I am Charlie," I added.

"What is your name?" my wife asked.

"My name is Prisha," the girl replied shyly, avoiding eye contact as she spoke.

"Prisha, you are beautiful," my wife said. "We're just here to love you, spend time with you, and get to know you. We want you to know that we don't judge you in any way. We just want to learn about your life."

We learned that Prisha's entire family was killed in a large earthquake that hit in 2015. Prisha eventually ended up here, enslaved by this darkness. But what she really wanted to do in life was become a beautician.

The lights flickered, then faded to black. There was a power outage in the block of rooms we were meeting in. We walked outside to sit at a public table that had working lights. We spotted a nearby awning that suited our need, and we began walking quickly to avoid the pouring rain. Prisha, however, didn't seem to be in a hurry. She was walking slowly and gazing up at the sky.

"Prisha," I asked, after we sat down, "why were you looking up into the sky?"

"Well," she explained, "I wanted to enjoy the sky. I've been locked in a room for six days straight and have been with at least ten customers per day. Today is the first day this week that I have left that room, to meet with you all. So, like I said, I just wanted to enjoy the sky."

Her words pierced our hearts and grieved our souls. Deeply desiring that Prisha would know how dearly loved by God she is, we longed to do anything we could to help her!

As we sat down under the awning, my eyes were drawn to a tattoo on the inside of Prisha's forearm. The tattoo read FAITH, HOPE, LOVE in an intriguing design. I thought, *Why in the world would a girl like this have a tattoo that says FAITH, HOPE, LOVE? I have to ask!*

"That is a really cool tattoo," I said. "Why did you decide to get it?"

"I thought the design looked cool," Prisha replied with a smile.

"I agree the design is really nice; I think it is such a great tattoo. Do you know the meaning of it?"

"No, I don't know," Prisha responded.

I began thinking, *Could God have put this tattoo into Prisha's life as a bridge to the gospel?*

"Prisha," I shared with excitement, "it is truly possible for you to have *love* and *hope* in your life."

"I really do want to experience faith, hope, and love," she replied. "I haven't felt those things since I lost my family."

"I know how you can experience them," I shared. "You will experience great *love* and great *hope* in your life if you first trust Jesus and have *faith* in Him."

As our conversation deepened, we discovered that Prisha was Buddhist. The Lord burned it into our hearts: we had to proclaim just how much Jesus loves Prisha! One problem: the rain was pounding down on the metal awning, forcing us to speak very loudly, and a hotel busboy along with a hotel guard stood nearby listening. They were intrigued by our conversation. Normally, I'd be thrilled for them to overhear the gospel being shared. But that wasn't such a good idea in this country. Sharing about Jesus was illegal, and too much was on the line for Prisha to jeopardize that. Tonight, we believed, was Prisha's night. We knew that we needed to talk to her about the peace Jesus could bring and wanted nothing to hinder that from happening.

I leaned over to Omar and whispered, "We need to get another hotel room so we can talk privately about Jesus with Prisha. Can you tell the hotel staff that it is too loud out here because of the rain and request a room temporarily?"

Omar talked to the hotel staff, and they granted our request. We ran through the pouring rain into our new meeting space, shutting and locking the door behind us. Our privacy once again protected, we shared about Jesus and encouraged Prisha to give her life to Him. She was moved by our conversation but not ready to pray verbally and commit to Christ in that moment.

"I want to follow Jesus," she said, "and I will do that when I get out of here and to the main city!"

We ended our time together by praying over Prisha. I do not remember exactly what we prayed, but I remember the moment being powerful. While Prisha did not commit her life to Christ in that moment, gospel seeds had been planted. It would now be up to God to grow them.

Before we left, Prisha said to us, "This is the first time I have felt like family with anyone since my family was killed in the earthquake. Thank you for giving me your love, wisdom, and active help." As we parted ways and drove away that night, we began thinking, praying, and strategizing how we might help get Prisha out of bondage and help her forward in her life.

The next morning, our friend received a message from Prisha that said, "I have never felt peace like this in my life before now."

It seemed the Spirit of God was up to something in Prisha! God was so concerned for Prisha that He had us leave home, travel halfway around the world, seek out specific connections for several days, and dive into mud puddles of human need—in this case, for one life: Prisha's. We have no idea how Prisha's story will end. But was the journey worth it? Absolutely!

Our one night with Prisha originated in a God-given burden poured out during a sermon one year prior. God was speaking and my wife, Dara, was intently listening as a man preached about the suffering people of the world and how God is calling us to fight for them! One year before, as the message concluded with prayer, Dara experienced a taste of God's heart for the trafficked and enslaved.

God gave my wife this burden, a piece of His very heart. And why would God do that? Because He cares for those like Prisha. God sees Prisha. He goes after just one. And He sends us with His heart—even, and perhaps *especially*, for the sake of one.

One of Jesus' followers named Luke reveals God's heart through the images of a sheep, a coin, and a son. Luke assures us that one dusty, dirty, scratched-up coin was worth seeking out (Luke 15:8–10). Dig further into Luke 15 yourself and you'll discover a father who decided that facing cultural shame to run out and meet his returning son was worth it.

These two passages (about the coin and the son) open up with a powerful picture of a blunt truth: Luke lets us know that Jesus will "leave the ninety-nine [sheep] in the open country and go after the *one* that is lost until he finds it . . . And when he has found it, he lays it on his shoulders, rejoicing!" (Luke 15:4–5 ESV, italics mine). To Jesus, just one is worth it. And *so* worth it that He will leave the other ninety-nine in open country—in danger of wolves, bears, or whatever else might come against them! It seems that God goes to extreme measures for the sake of the lost, even if it means endangering the lives of His followers on Earth, for the sake of His eternal plan. I love how Nik Ripken put it when preaching at the Finishing the Task Conference in 2017: "Jesus would sacrifice ninety-nine of us for one Isis, one Al-Qaeda, one Al-Shabaab!" Even one person is worth risking everything for.

I love the story of Desmond Doss portrayed in the movie *Hacksaw Ridge.* Desmond Doss was a combat medic in World War II. One night on the island of Okinawa when all others retreated, this soldier did not. He knew that there were more wounded and dying soldiers in desperate need of rescue. So he worked all night long and saved seventy-five men—one at a time. He ran back and forth across the battlefield, carrying out any and all soldiers who couldn't make it out on their own. The entire time, Desmond was praying, "Please, Lord, help me get one more! . . . one more! . . . help me get one more!"[1] Corporal Desmond Doss knew that just one person was worth risking everything for.

One dusty, dirty coin was worth it. One lost son was worth it. One sheep was worth it. One soldier was worth it. One single life is absolutely worth it—no matter how far you may have to run until you get to them, no matter how stuck in a mud puddle they are, and no matter how muddy you may need to get in bringing the love of Jesus to them. They are worth it!

Not only does Jesus say they are worth it, but He put His actions where His mouth was when He walked on Earth in human flesh: He went after the woman at the well as well as the woman caught in adultery, He went after twelve men who were living without purpose, He sought out Peter after He denied Him, and He risked everything for you and me by going to the cross! Time and time again, Jesus proclaims in word and deed: one is worth it. He endlessly went after the one. And He is still going after *ones* through people like you and me!

Sometimes you might have to seek after one person, even

when it seems they are running further and further off into thick mud puddles! They aren't coming on their own. They need someone to chase them down, pick them up, bring them to the racetrack of kingdom life, and then rejoice over their life.

The shepherd went after his one sheep when it ran off the other direction—and who knows how far or fast he had to go! The shepherd picked that sheep up, put it on his shoulders, and brought it back, rejoicing. Will you pursue others the same way Jesus, the Good Shepherd, has pursued you? Even if they keep running? Even if they don't budge at first?

Is there one person your Shepherd desires to seek out through you? There are more Prishas in the world, waiting for someone to seek them out, chase them down, and bring them to His kingdom. Is just one life worth it to you?

Now What?

- Are you willing to risk for the sake of one person? Why or why not?
- Who is one person God might want you to chase down with His love?
- Pray now, asking God to give you a taste of His heart for the lost and lonely of the world, even if it is just one person.

TWENTY-ONE

STRANGERS

IT WAS my first trip to the bush of East Africa. Our team drove from place to place in an open-back Land Cruiser. The dust was incredible. After several long journeys, we were covered in dusty, dirty grime from head to toe.

We stopped in a small town in the middle of nowhere. The town may have been nowhere, but the people were everywhere; the local, open-air market was jam-packed. Maasai tribals were funneling in from every direction. Venders lined the dirt street with table after table of goods to sell.

The Land Cruiser came to a halt, and I jumped out to stretch my legs as the driver began a conversation with one of the locals. I decided to look around a bit. That decision was easier said than done. Getting thirty feet through the mob came at the expense of jostling, twisting, and contorting. Twenty-five feet in, I decided to reverse course back to the truck. When I got to the place we parked, the truck was gone. I looked left, right, then in every direction. No truck. No familiar faces. The Land Cruiser and our team were nowhere to be found.

Fear immediately filled my pounding heart! My mind quickly flooded with one thought after another: *Where did they go? Do they*

*know I am not in the vehicle? I literally have nothing with me! I have
no clue where we are! No one here speaks English! I am completely lost.
This cannot be good!*

I decided to make my way down the street and attempt to
communicate with someone (anyone!) that I was looking for a
truck with foreigners. The first several attempts were a disaster. I
wasn't connecting in a meaningful way with anyone. Then I
noticed a Maasai man and approached him. I moved my hands left
and right as if I was gripping a steering wheel and driving a car. I
even made truck sounds, like kids do when they're pretending to
drive. I'm sure I looked like a completely crazy person. I'm pretty
sure the Massai guy thought so; he looked at me like I had a few
loose screws. I thought to myself, *Well, at least, he'll have a story to
tell and laugh at for days to come.*

I felt like I was playing a game of charades; only this was no
longer a game. Scouring my mind for any way to connect, I
recalled the Swahili word *Mzungu* (which means "white person").
As if I was trying to beat the game timer, I blurted out to the man,
"Mzungu!" His head nodding in affirmation, he repeated the word
back to me as he pointed down the road. Two or three similar
conversations along the way confirmed I was heading in the right
direction.

Finally, I emerged from an opening in the crowd and saw the
truck and team! I exhaled a great sigh of relief. Reassurance and
peace flooded my soul. A little embarrassed, I didn't want to tell
the team how lost I really felt, so I just hopped in the truck and
acted as if everything was normal. They seemed to buy it, and we
were on our way.

This was not the only time I felt lost or alone in another country. I remember landing in a local airport on my first trip to
China. As I exited the plane, I looked for signs in English. Not a
single one existed; all the signs were Chinese symbols. And not one
person spoke a word of English either. Or if they did, they didn't
want to use it.

After walking through every inch of the airport, I found the
baggage area. I waited for my luggage and then walked outside the

airport doors to navigate my next adventure: a taxi ride. A cab pulled up, and I got in. I handed the driver a business card with an address in Chinese. That was all I had with me to meet a contact somewhere in the city. I was hoping (and praying) he would get me to the right place. After a twenty-minute drive, he did. I was grateful.

On another occasion, I walked the streets of China alone. Although people bustled to and fro, the world in front of me felt empty and lonely. I was a stranger in a faraway land. Alone, unable to properly communicate, and sticking out like a sore thumb, it's crazy what feeling like a lost stranger can do to you. Life can be difficult to navigate when we don't fit in.

These "lost and alone" stories remind me that, like being a stranger in a foreign land, those who believe in Jesus are strangers to this world. In fact, we are only passing through. And the reality of the world we live in is grim. It is not as it should be—violence, suicide, family division, racism, war, starvation, disease, slavery, trafficking, and death run rampant.

We really are strangers and foreigners in this land we call Earth. We live as citizens of another kingdom, embrace another way of life, and follow another leader who's in charge: King Jesus. We are not destined to stay here as believers but to be reunited with God face to face when His kingdom fully comes! In fact, those who lived by faith throughout the Scriptures saw themselves as strangers too:

> [They admitted] that they were foreigners and
> strangers on earth. People who say such things
> show that they are looking for a country of their
> own. If they had been thinking of the country they
> had left, they would have had opportunity to
> return. Instead, they were longing for a better
> country—a heavenly one. Therefore God is not
> ashamed to be called their God, for he has
> prepared a city for them. (Hebrews
> 11:13–16 NIV)

Whenever we do not fit in or we feel like strangers among others, we must remember we actually *are* strangers and that our one goal on Earth is to reveal the person of Jesus through our lives (1 Peter 2:11–12). I once heard it said by evangelist Adrian Despres, "God must be a horrible ogre to leave us in a world like this. Except for one thing: mission."

Feeling (and at times being) rejected, sidelined, and ignored are unfortunately the reality of strangers. I have experienced this reality from time to time. And maybe, like me, you have felt that way too. It is quite a lonely reality to experience. But it is also an amazing opportunity to remember that Earth is only our temporary shelter and that our heavenly home will one day be our permanent residence.

Right now, we currently have a foretaste of our heavenly home through God's Spirit (2 Corinthians 5:5; Romans 8:23). When we are pushed and pressed and feeling like we are running this race alone, we must remember that the Father, Son, and Holy Spirit have all three made their home *in* us right now (John 14:23–26). And their presence in us is only a small taste of our home to come!

Maybe you are currently feeling lost and lonely in the race. Maybe you're running a leg of the race no one else is running. Sometimes God allows others to separate themselves from us (and even desert us altogether) so that we can be more at home with Him than we are at home with the world. God is constantly providing us opportunity to affirm the truth of these well-known lyrics: "I have decided to follow Jesus . . . / Though none go with me, still I will follow . . . / No turning back, no turning back."

Although it may not be easy to live as a stranger in our world, have you discovered the amazing reality of being *at home* with Jesus? Allow your circumstances to drive you more and more to Jesus as He makes His home with you—and as you make your home with Him. And as you do, ponder this: whatever "home" you build with Jesus on Earth will only be a small taste of the reality of your heavenly home to come!

Now What?

- When was a time you have felt like a stranger: lost, alone, misunderstood?
- Read Colossians 3:1–4. How can you allow the feelings of being a "stranger" drive you to fix your eyes more and more on heavenly things?
- Starting this week, how will you seek to be more at home with Jesus than with worldly satisfaction?

TWENTY-TWO

WHEN PRAYERS EXPLODE LIKE BALLOONS

BEFORE I TOOK my first trip to the Hadzabe tribe of East Africa, I continued to pray, *Lord, bring me a burden bearer, an Amos.* The name Amos in the Bible means burden bearer: to carry God's heart and burden for a people or place. So I prayed, *Lord will you bring me someone who will carry your heart for the Hadzabe people? Will you bring me someone I can train and partner with to see your kingdom advance among the Hadzabe?*

During this first scouting trip, I ventured to a village to preach the gospel; I wanted to see how responsive or open the Hadzabe people might be to Jesus. Various tribals responded, and some asked for prayer. One man requested prayer for the pain he was experiencing in his knee.

I asked him, "What is your name?"

His response surprised and rattled me. "My name is Amos," he replied.

Did God really bring me a burden bearer with the very name Amos?! I thought. I expected to find someone with the right heart. I never expected God to provide someone with the same exact name. We prayed for the pain in Amos's knee. After that I pulled him aside to discuss the burden God had placed on my heart.

Amos had said yes to following Jesus when I shared with him. So I asked, "If I return, would you be interested in learning Bible stories and being trained to go and share about Jesus with more Hadzabe people?"

"Yes," Amos replied, "I would be very interested in doing that!"

All signs seemed to be pointing to an answered prayer! My heart swelled with joy and pounded with excitement. I praised God for His provision that seemed to land right in my lap!

A year later, I returned as planned to the Hadzabe, along with my friend Nathan. Together Nathan and I began training Amos and his wife, Olo. We taught them Bible stories nearly every day for weeks and weeks. We prayed together, ate together, and spent precious time together. It seemed everything was going as we had planned. It seemed we had found a mudrunner among the Hadzabe people!

But things don't always go as planned. Things aren't always as they seem. Several months after having returned to the States from this trip, our friend and ministry partner, Mary, called from Africa. One of our great African friends, Oya, had died. Upon hearing the news, I immediately wrote this prayer update:

Our friend Oya recently became very sick and died. Oya, a Hadza hunter, was a middle-aged father, husband, man of joy, and a central character to his village. He will be missed by many. He did hear the gospel before he died and listened to many stories from God's Word—I would say he even hungered to hear stories from the Bible. Pray with us for Oya's family and village. Lord have mercy.

WE LOVED OYA. What's more, we really liked him! Oya was like the "class clown" of his village. We always enjoyed his company, and he often made us laugh.

A year after receiving the news about Oya's death, Nathan and I returned to the Hadzabe village. One of the first things we did was ask Mary more about Oya and his death. "Mary, what really happened to Oya?" I inquired. "Why did he really die? What sickness did he get?"

Mary's eyes sank toward the ground. "Well," she said, "we have heard that Amos was practicing witchcraft. Amos became angry with Oya and placed a curse on him."

"What?!" I exclaimed. I was simultaneously dumbfounded and angered. "How is this possible? What happened to Amos? Where is he now?"

"The villagers chased him out," Mary explained. "He went to live in the next village over."

Hardly allowing Mary to finish her sentence, I pressed further: "And what happened to him there?"

She told us all she knew: "Amos had a conflict with a witch doctor in that village. So he killed the witch doctor. The people ran him out of that village too."

"This is crazy; I cannot believe this has happened," I said. "Where is Amos now?"

"We heard that Amos went to a third village," Mary answered. "While he was there, he stole some food from someone and ate it. Soon after, his belly began swelling up. It swelled so much that it became as big and tight as an overfilled balloon. His stomach eventually exploded open and Amos died."

I could hardly believe what I was hearing. Apparently, Amos did not just begin dabbling in witchcraft after we left but had been fully engaged in it all along. He was living a double life of deceit and selfish gain. I could not help but think of Judas's gut bursting open after his deceitful life that led to his demise (John 12:6; Acts 1:18) or of Acts 5:1–10 where a man named Ananias deceived the community of believers. It says that he lied to the Spirit of God, and as a result he was struck down dead. God's judgment took care of that bad egg.

Could that be what happened to Amos? I'm not certain, but maybe. Could he have reaped what he sowed unto judgment very literally (Galatians 6:7–8)? Possibly. Whether Amos's death came by judgment, coincidence, or as a result of his numbered days simply running out (Psalm 139:16), God was working all things out for His purposes and plans.

At first I began thinking to myself, *I thought Amos was the answer to prayer! Not only did he explode, but so did my so-called answered prayer! What is the deal with this?!* But as time went on, I realized that God was in it all along. His ways are higher than my ways. I still do not understand the fullness of Amos, his death, and our interactions. Nor do I understand why everything happened as it did. What I do know is that God used Amos to bring me back to the Hadzabe with a strong vision. God used my initial interactions with Amos to build my faith and fuel me to forge forward. God simply had other plans for who would become the true burden bearer among the Hadzabe people.

Little did I know, God had already brought a burden bearer who was with us from the beginning. It just wasn't who I initially thought it was. The true burden bearer was already running the race alongside us, and she was already catching the vision to embrace all the mud puddles of great need around her. It was Mary. Mary was the burden-bearing *Amos* all along. And God has confirmed His choice to me again and again over time.

We may pray and pray and pray. And we may think we know how God is answering our prayers. We might later find out that our answered prayers seem to explode like balloons and leave us shocked, taken off guard, confused, and disappointed. But that is hardly the end of it. God is doing more than we could ever ask or imagine (Ephesians 3:20). And His answers to our prayers are far better than we can see, scheme, or dream up.

Our current situation may not seem better than we could imagine in the moment. But in the fullness of time—when all is said and done—God's sovereign answers will accomplish so much more. In fact, they will utterly amaze us! (Habakkuk 1:5). We cannot forget that we run this race "by faith, not by sight" (2 Corinthians 5:7 NIV). Trust Him. Trust His faithfulness. He will come through—often in unimaginable ways!

Now What?

- Looking back at your life up to this point, when was a time that you can now see God was doing far more than you imagined?
- What would it look like for you to trust God's ways more than your own in the midst of uncertainty and the unseen?
- What do you think burdens or breaks God's heart in the world? Pray and ask God to give you a taste of what burdens Him, a taste of what breaks His heart in the world.

TWENTY-THREE

RUNNING SUSTENANCE

I JOLTED AWAKE—SWEATY and heart pounding. I was relieved it was only a dream, yet I couldn't help but wonder, *Is there more to this?* In my dream Jesus was deformed with old, crinkly skin. He was far more decrepit and disturbing than the healthy vision of a thirty-year-old Middle Eastern carpenter that you might imagine. I was caught off guard and unsettled. Before I could even begin to make sense of the dream, these words—as if from Jesus Himself—came to mind: "That is how these people see me."

The people here have a view of Jesus that is completely skewed! I thought. *They desperately need Him, but they do not know the resurrected Jesus who is full of life!*

I walked to the main room and breakfast was served: freshly picked salad with some seriously spicy peppers from the backyard garden. This was not my typical breakfast, but I was grateful for the hospitality of this Central Asian Muslim family who allowed us to stay in their home.

When I finished breakfast, I headed toward the soccer field on the other side of the village where our team was running a soccer camp for local children. As I made my way to join them, many villagers shuffled past me. They were heading toward the town mosque down the street. A loudspeaker echoed out, "Allahu Akbar," as the call to prayer began with volume enough for everyone in the town to hear and heed.

I took note of the impoverished community's rundown and neglected buildings left over from the past horrors of communism. Statues of Stalin and Lenin remained standing but were crumbling at the edges and overgrown with weeds. They had clearly been abandoned for some time. The statues and buildings felt like a symbolic outward reality of the people's inward souls: dusty, dilapidated, downcast; crumbling apart and hoping for something better that never came.

I reached the soccer field and connected with the team. It wasn't long before a crowd of children from the village joined us and began playing the game of "futball" they love so much.

As they played, one boy particularly caught our eye—Vladik. It wasn't his soccer skills that set him apart (although he was pretty good!); it was his varied skin and hair color. They signaled his lower-class status in this particular country; in fact, many people despised Vladik's ethnic background. Still, there was something more drawing us to him.

Between games we began a conversation with Vladik. We discovered he had not yet met Jesus. We shared the basic story of Jesus, and Vladik joyfully responded and placed his trust in the Lord! Vladik's face lit up with a smile that reflected the light of heaven. Vladik may have been considered lower-class by his country, but he had now become a son of the most high God! From second-class citizen to firstborn privilege, from least and last to child of the King—God's favor shone on Vladik.

He said, "You all are like my moms and dads." We were deeply moved by this young boy and the undeniable joy in his eyes. I wondered how many people had overlooked him due to his social status, age, and geography. We hadn't even parted ways, and I was already missing him! I couldn't quit rejoicing over the fact that his life had been changed for eternity.

We gave Vladik a children's Bible in his own language. He

clung to it like it was gold. I'm quite certain the world's greatest wrestler couldn't have pried that Bible from Vladik's grip. He just kept holding the Bible tight against his chest and near to his heart.

When our time together ended, Vladik clutched his Bible tightly in his hand and sprinted toward home. He was so excited to share with his family what had happened. I was amazed by Vladik's hunger for the Word of God. Finally, Vladik had the chance to begin learning about the living Jesus for himself.

Unfortunately, many do not yet have Vladik's opportunity. They do not have anyone to tell them about Jesus. Nor do they have access to a Bible they can possess or understand. And if they wanted one, they wouldn't even have the slightest clue of where to begin to find one. Right now, this is what John 3:16 looks like in many languages:

"   "

It simply doesn't exist. Sadly, this is still the reality for many people groups all around the globe. Until recently it was the case for the Hadzabe tribe of East Africa. That is, until we completed translating and orally recording Bible stories into their isolated click language.

The work was painstaking, but oh was it worth it! I will never forget the day Onwas, a Hadzabe tribal elder, heard the Scriptures in his language for the first time. As he listened to the stories, he was filled with joy and began to repeat (quite loudly!) every word he heard! He declared that he finally understood the stories of God. The impact of God's Word in his life and many others was astounding.

Onwas proclaimed, "I am so happy to hear the Word of God in my language. I believe that if Hadzabe people hear these words, they will go to God! As I listen in Hadzabe language, I understand all the words. Now, I always think about Jesus and God rather than the sun god, Ishoko, who we have traditionally worshiped. I was always thinking of Ishoko in the morning and asking for his help in my hunting. But now, it is always God and Jesus I seek."

All Onwas needed was one small taste of God's Word to leave him with an insatiable hunger for more and more! The Hadzabe are master honey collectors. And when they find a honey source, they joyfully celebrate. That said, I had never seen Onwas nearly as excited for any amount of honey as he was when the Word of God became accessible to him in his own language.

Another tribal member was given the Hadzabe audio Bible. He sat down under a tree and listened intently to every word. I thought he might stop after an hour or so. Not even close. He continued well into the night, listening to book after book of the Bible. He was hooked.

In another remote village, tribals came for days to hear the Word of God. We would share God's Word with them for hours each day. To our amazement, they kept coming and pleading with us to share more and more. They could hardly wait to wake up and join us. Day after day, they couldn't wait to hear another story of what God had to say. They hungered for God's Word so much that they willingly and sacrificially left behind their everyday necessities to come and listen.

As my mind races to those like Vladik, Onwas, and countless others who truly hunger for God's Word, I am compelled to evaluate my own interactions with the Scriptures. What would my life be like without a Bible; would it look any different than it does now? What if I could not get my hands on a Bible even if I wanted to?

I am blessed to have the Bible easily accessible—anywhere at any time. I can read any of the various copies on my shelf, both at home and in my office. I can pull it up on my phone. I can search for it online. I can compare different versions and consult commentaries.

Such easy access to the Bible is nearly unfathomable to many people around the globe, such as my Somali friend John. The simple act of being seen with a Bible in Somalia, let alone professing faith in Jesus Christ, could get you killed. One day

John's family discovered that he had decided to leave Islam for Jesus, so they attempted to have him killed. John fled Somalia and upon arriving in a neighboring country, he sent me a picture of a Bible with the words, "Finally, I can have it! I cannot stop reading it. I have been spending hours in the Bible!" In a time when the shadow of death loomed over John, the Scriptures were life-giving and sustaining. This was the first time in years that John could freely places his hands on a paper copy of the Scriptures.

As available as the Bible is to me, I have to ask: do I hunger for God's Word as much as those who are hearing it with fresh ears or those willing to suffer greatly for it? I often fear that it's too easy for me to take the Word of God for granted. I imagine the same may be true for you.

To Vladik, Scripture was "more desirable than gold" (Psalm 19:10 NLT). To Onwas, Scripture was "sweeter than honey" (Psalm 19:10 NLT). To the tribals in a remote village, Scripture was more permanent and lasting than their mud huts would ever be (1 Peter 1:24–25), more filling than any food that a day of farming could ever provide (Psalm 81:10), and more empowering for God's work than any other power source (2 Timothy 3:16–17). To the man under the tree, Scripture was more reviving to his soul than any conversation or walk in the bush could provide (Psalm 19:7). To John, Scripture was life's very sustenance (Matthew 3:3). What is the Scripture to you?

To run a race well, a runner needs to be properly sustained with the right amount of nutrition. God's Word is nutrition to our soul. We must eat and drink it often to run the race God desires us to run.

A recent study by the Center for Bible Engagement found that those who read the Bible four or more times a week (compared to those who read the Bible less than four times a week) had significantly decreased loneliness, significantly increased victory over sin struggles (such as anger, bitterness in relationships, pornography, drunkenness, sex outside of marriage, etc.), and significant increases in sharing the gospel and discipling others. If we want to live and thrive as mudrunners, we must not "live by bread alone, but by every word that comes from the mouth of God" (Matthew 4:4 ᴇsᴠ). The Bible not only teaches us how to run well but points us to our running companion Himself, Jesus (John 5:39–40).

Evangelist Adrian Despres said, "Two things will last forever: people and God's Word. Invest your life in those two things!" Are you ready to invest in God's Word? His Word will last. His Word is sweet, reviving, and refreshing. His word is convicting, equipping, and life-giving. Why would we possibly wait?

Now What?

- Pray now and ask God, *Will you increase my hunger for Your Word? I want more.* Then commit to spending time regularly with God in His Word. As you read, consider following the simple, *nutritious* method described below to dig into His Word.
- Choose a book of the Bible to read through, one passage per day. If you are not sure where to begin, I recommend starting with Mark, then Acts, and then Ephesians. As you read a passage of the Bible each day, engage the following: **Head:** What is the passage saying? (What is the main message? Who are the characters; what do I learn about them? How do I see God at work; what do I learn about God—the Father, Jesus, the Holy Spirit—or about people, Satan or evil, etc.?) **Heart:** How did this story impact me? What is God speaking to me? (What part of the passage sticks out to me? What changes do I need to make in my beliefs, attitudes, or actions?) **Hands:** This very week, how will I practically obey what God has shown me? (What next step will I take?) **Feet:** Who will I share with? (Is there anyone in my life that I need to tell about what I learned in this passage?)
- Why not give it a try right now?

TWENTY-FOUR

BRIDGES OR BARRIERS

"WHY DO you always carry your weapon?" our friend Pascali asked as he pointed to my Bible. Pascali had invited us for a time of tea. So I, along with Nathan, Mary, and a pastor-translator named Simon, crammed into Pascali's small home together with his wife and children. Finding room for us all to sit was a chore.

"You are right," I said with excitement in a way that might lead the conversation to deeper places. "It is a spiritual weapon. I carry it around because we are teaching people the way of Jesus, and it all comes from God's Word to us. I read the Bible because it teaches me more about who Jesus is, it changes my life, and it brings me peace."

"You know, I myself am not a man of God," Pascali confessed.

"Well, why not?" I responded. "We are friends, so you can share with us freely. We do not condemn you."

Pascali reached into his pocket and slowly pulled something out. "It's because of this," he said, revealing a box of cigarettes.

Half shocked, I replied, "Pascali, cigarettes can't keep you from having a relationship with Jesus. Simply come to Him and trust Him. You cannot change your heart on your own. You cannot clean yourself up and then come to Jesus. You need to come to Jesus *first*, and then He will change your life as you come.

"Now, if Jesus asks you to give up your cigarettes once you begin following Him, well then, you better do it. But cigarettes can never stop you from coming to Him."

Simon, who had been translating up to this point, abruptly interjected, "I will not have such words come out of my mouth! This man certainly cannot come to Jesus unless he gives up his cigarettes. He cannot even touch them!"

Simon's words struck a nerve in me. I was fuming. I pointed my finger at Simon and commanded, "You can go ahead and keep your mouth shut!"

I took in a deep breath to calm myself, then turned to Mary and asked, "Will you please translate this message to Pascali?"

Mary graciously shared. Pascali heard the message but was still sorting through Simon's contradicting words. Confused, Pascali was not ready to follow Jesus. My heart sank with sadness, anger, and frustration.

As we walked away from Pascali's home, my mind was reeling: *How dare anyone put up boundaries to Jesus! Pascali is so close to Jesus yet thinks he must do all these things before he can even get to Jesus. What a lie! Simon will be held responsible for this!*

Jesus' words to the Pharisees connected with me like never before:

> [The Pharisees] tie up heavy, cumbersome loads and
> put them on other people's shoulders, but they
> themselves are not willing to lift a finger to move
> them. . . . "Woe to you, teachers of the law and
> Pharisees, you hypocrites! You shut the kingdom
> of heaven in people's faces. You yourselves do not
> enter, nor will you let those enter who are trying
> to. Woe to you, teachers of the law and
> Pharisees, you hypocrites! You travel over land
> and sea to win a single convert, and when you
> have succeeded, you make them twice as much a

child of hell as you are." (Matthew 23:4,
13–15 NIV)

"You shut the kingdom of heaven in people's faces." That is quite an intense statement. And in the moment, I felt the fullness of it. Simon had slammed the door of the kingdom right in Pascali's face.

Jesus was not just trying to provoke or point his finger in the face of the Pharisees for the fun of it. He was defending the downtrodden, people like Pascali, people who desperately needed hope. The Pharisees were building barriers, not bridges. They were shutting people out of the kingdom and placing heavy spiritual burdens on them. Jesus wasn't having it. He wanted more for people than impossible obstacles to climb over and impenetrable doors to try and knock down. Jesus came to break down these barriers and build them into bridges.

As frustrated as I was with Simon, I was equally convicted by the Lord. He reminded me that I had often been the one building barriers rather than bridges. I couldn't help but think of all the times I'd ignored and disregarded others, argued with people, looked down on those not like me, tore down people who opposed me, and let pride in my position stake claim over humble servanthood—all while claiming to be a follower of Jesus.

I have asked the Lord to forgive me. And graciously He has. Praise Him for the cross! My heart longs to be more and more like Jesus, building bridges to the Pascalis of the world. I often pray that Jesus will use me to build more bridges than barriers throughout the course of my life.

Do you need to go to the Lord and confess that you've been building more barriers than bridges? What would it look like to begin building bridges for Jesus' sake?

Maybe you relate more to Pascali's story of barriers built between you and Jesus. Maybe the door to God's forgiveness and grace hasn't been opened to you but has actually been slammed in your face. If that's your story, I am truly sorry. The good news is, there is still hope for you, as God is still waiting with open arms—

door wide open—for you to receive His invitation of forgiveness and love.

The day we walked away from Pascali's home was not the last time we saw him. We returned a year later and continued our conversation about Jesus. Still, Pascali was not ready. Among other things, Jesus and alcohol weren't going to mix very well for Pascali. He shared openly that he had a drinking problem. He was often drunk, getting into village fights, and struggling to provide for his family. We assured him we would pray and that Jesus was there to help. We left him with our heartfelt prayer and desire: "We hope you will come to know Jesus by the time we see you again!"

A year later, we returned. When we met Pascali, he was beaming with excitement. "Do you remember what you told me one year ago?" he asked. "Well, two weeks ago I became born again! Jesus has helped me quit drinking and begin providing for my family!" Joy radiated from Pascali's face. Finally, a bridge to Pascali had been built, and it made all the difference.

Pascali's wife acknowledged God's work and transformation in him. "It is true," she affirmed. "Pascali is a changed man. He loves more intentionally. He provides for our family. He is even spending time with our children. Praise God!"

Stop building barriers. Become a bridge builder. It's worth it! There are so many Pascalis in the world who need a bridge to the message and person of Jesus. Jesus is worthy of our bridge-building efforts. In fact, He's counting on us as we join His mission of seeking and saving the lost (Luke 19:10).

Now What?

- Have your actions resembled more of a bridge builder or barrier builder? How so?
- Do you need to confess any acts of barrier building to the Lord and ask His forgiveness? Do so now.
- What steps can you take to become an active bridge builder for God's kingdom?

TWENTY-FIVE

WHEN THE ROPE RUNS OUT

WE WERE SURROUNDED. By the time we had woken up and exited our tent, scores of people (most we knew, some we didn't) filled our campsite and were waiting for us. Word had spread throughout the village that Nathan and I were departing that morning. Accompanying the news was a plan to meet at our camp.

They were gathering for one reason: a parting gift. Not for us, for them. Let me explain. Due to customs established by anthropologists, linguists, *National Geographic* researchers, other various cultural and scientific researchers, and tourists, Hadzabe had come to expect that all "guests" would give villagers good gifts upon leaving the village. Now that we were leaving, the villagers came to collect their gifts. And believe me, when tribals think there might be gifts involved, they start coming out of the woodwork. So much so, you begin to wonder, *Just where are they all coming from?!*

There we were, not quite sure what to do. The entire village was encircling us, demanding gifts. Money and missions can be tricky. We learned the hard way previous times that giving gifts of money—even to seemingly trustworthy people—often leads to an entire village getting blasted drunk for as many days as the money will last them. In that setting, it's amazing how long a single dollar might stretch.

We were at a loss for words. We didn't really have much of anything to offer them. The tribals took notice of our hesitancy. And when we weren't readily giving them what they wanted, the crowd began to stir and murmur.

A man from the back raised his voice and demanded, "Give us twenty thousand shillings for your time here!"

The amount wasn't unreasonable. We just knew the results would be far from desirable if we gave into their demand.

So we responded, "We have shared with you all along. We gave you audio Bibles. We helped you understand God's Word. I mean, we brought you the very Word of God. Isn't that enough?"

Apparently, it was not enough! And apparently, this was not the best statement to make. Smiles dropped and tension rose. All of a sudden, the air felt thick. People were clearly displeased. Some young men began riling up the crowd against us. They happened to be the same young men who had begged us to buy them marijuana from a neighboring tribe when we were out hunting with them just days before. Maybe this was their chance to squeeze something out of us.

The yelling continued. The kind faces we had shared life with for so many days disappeared. While their anger escalated, my fear elevated.

I looked to our friend Mary for help. "Mary, what are they saying?" I asked in desperation.

"They are saying that they will tell all Hadzabe villages that you are terrible people," she answered, "that no one should trust you, and that they will shoot arrows at your car and pop out all your tires."

This was not good. A single moment was about to rob the validity of our entire ministry among the Hadzabe people. After so much preparation and work, we couldn't go down like this. I felt like our luck had run out—like everything was hanging on by a tiny thread and ready to snap. We had to smooth out the situation. Something had to be done. But what?

Suddenly, an idea came to mind. I believe the Holy Spirit rescued us by providing wisdom that could have only come from God. I spoke up, "We are very sorry. We do not want to offend you. So we will give you the twenty thousand shillings you have asked for . . . in corn flour. We will make sure to give you twenty thousand shillings worth of corn flour because you have said you are in great need; this should help you feed yourselves and your young children."

The older generation was pleased. The young men were silenced. Everyone's hunger would be filled. God's grace broke through. This was certainly not the first time, nor the last.

Whether I have been at the end of my rope or have made blatant blunders and mistakes, there have been many times I have needed God's grace to break through. Like the time I tried to share a message from God's Word with a village of tribal people and then asked them to give a prayerful response.

And oh what a response they gave! "We are hungry. We want to make food for us and the children. Are you finished? Can we go now?"

I felt embarrassed and deflated. That was certainly not the response I was looking for nor expecting. I was trying to make something happen, and it became apparent that it was not at the right moment nor in the right way.

Then there was the time a woman left her baby and ran off. This woman had begun to follow Jesus and seemed deeply impacted by the Lord. Next thing we know, she left her young baby on Mary's doorstep and disappeared into the bush. What do you do with a situation like that?! I was clueless. What kind of field manual trains you for situations like that? All I could do was ask God for another breakthrough of His grace.

As mudrunners, we will often find that we are at the end of ourselves. We can so easily become burdened and weighed down by failures that hit close to home or by circumstances that are far beyond our ability. We will discover that the obstacles in the race are far beyond us. We will find that we don't really have what it takes in and of ourselves. But could it be that's right where God wants us? Could it be that God desires us to face situations where not only have we hit the end of our rope but the rope is long gone? Check out what Paul the apostle wrote when his rope ran out: "We were under great pressure, far beyond our ability to endure, so that we despaired of life itself. Indeed, we felt we had received the sentence of death. But this happened that we might not rely on ourselves but on God, who raises the dead" (2 Corinthians 1:8–9 NIV).

Looking back, I am actually grateful for the times when I have hit the end of my rope, faced unknowns, experienced failure, and called out to God in absolute desperation. Why? It is in those places that I have truly experienced the fullness of God's grace. At the end of my rope I found the beginning of God's favor, provision, power, and pleasure in my life—regardless of what I can or cannot do.

While God may want us to reach the end of our ropes to realize our utter need for dependence on Him, I don't believe He desires to leave us in our despair. Take another look at what Paul declares:

> He has delivered us from such a deadly peril, and he will deliver us again. On him we have set our hope that he will continue to deliver us. (2 Corinthians 1:10 NIV)

> I will boast all the more gladly of my weaknesses, so that the power of Christ may rest upon me. For the sake of Christ, then, I am content with weaknesses, insults, hardships, persecutions, and calamities. For when I am weak, then I am strong (2 Corinthians 12:9–10 ESV).

While the powerful grace of God meets us in our desperation, it does not leave us in our despair. Jesus wants us to realize our weakness and desperate need for Him so that we depend on Him. Depending on Jesus gives us the opportunity to witness

His incredible power to deliver us and move us forward in strength.

True grace never causes passivity but power and provision to execute His will. Take a look at every time *grace* appears in Scripture; empowered action always follows. Our weakness becomes strength when it meets God's grace. God provides us what is needed in order to do what is wanted by Him. What amazing, empowering, and provisionary grace!

That said, we often don't discover God's grace until we face insurmountable odds. That's exactly what we experienced when God's grace broke through that time we were surrounded by tribals who were demanding money from us. When the odds seemed impossible and the solution unsolvable, God provided a way forward.

I once heard a preacher illustrate it this way: a small man was drowning in the ocean. He was absolutely terrified. Seven strong men ran to his rescue. Even then, it took more than thirty minutes to save him. If only two or three had come to his rescue, this small man would have grabbed them, pulled them down, and drowned them along with himself. The man—desperate, realizing he was powerless and in great need—possessed immense strength. Out of his weakness, he was strong.

So go ahead. Next time you face impossibility, look for God's grace. Next time you face despair, look for His grace. Next time you fail, grace. Next time you hit the end of your rope, grace.

As our ropes run out and we are caught up in His grace, we will find His very strength moving us forward. And as we move forward by His empowering grace, we cannot forget those in need of the very grace we have tasted. We cannot forget those who are slipping in mud, tripping up, and not feeling like they measure up. We cannot forget those around us who are falling, grasping for something secure to hold onto, in absolute desperation. If we know the power of God's grace, we must radically extend this rescuing grace so that others can experience its power too.

Ominous feelings filled my heart as I walked the streets of a city in China. A stranger walked up to me and attempted to communicate something in Chinese. It didn't take long to discover that he could not speak a word of English, and I could not speak a word of Chinese. The language gap didn't stop him. He kept trying to tell me something as he held up two fingers in the shape of a cross.

We happened to be standing near a building with a cross on it, and he motioned for me to follow him in, so I did. I looked around and found a young girl who knew English and Chinese, and asked her, "Can you tell me what this man has been trying to say?"

She listened to him and then translated for us. "He is asking, 'Do you know Jesus? Do you need a Bible? Do you need food? And do you need money for a place to stay?'"

I remember thinking, *We must look like we really need Jesus in our lives and that we look lost and don't know what we're doing!* (and let's face it: in reality, most of those things are true in one way or another).

To be honest, His Christlike actions floored me. This Chinese man had sought to radically extend God's grace by sharing the most important message in the world while also making sure perfect strangers were welcomed and had all their needs met.

I joined my new friend and brother for a meal at a nearby soup kitchen. With the help of the young girl's translating, I thanked him for his kindness and let him know that I had provisions for all my needs. I imagine this man understood what it was like to be thrown into situations far beyond his ability. I imagine this man's desperation had collided with God's empowering grace. I imagine he was simply, gratefully, and lovingly doing all he could to pay it forward.

What if there were more people who lived that way? I dream of an army of believers freed of all the guilt and shame of their former failures, believers who have been gripped by grace at the end of their ropes, believers who surge forward with unimaginable strength. I dream of an army of believers who live as conduits for God's grace in everyday spaces and places. Can you dream and imagine with me? Imagine what could happen in a world filled with grace-filled, grace-giving Jesus lovers!

Mudrunners don't only *need* God's grace, they *live* by God's grace. It is their very strength.

Now What?

- When was a time that your "rope ran out," leaving you in utter desperation? What happened? Did you reach out to Jesus or attempt to move forward by your own strength?
- Have you ever noticed that in the Scriptures empowered obedience and victory always follow grace? Check out Ephesians 2:8–10 and 1 Corinthians 15:10. What might happen in your life if you received the fullness of God's grace?
- Do you need to receive God's grace or somehow extend His grace in new ways? What would that look like?

TWENTY-SIX

RADICAL SHELTER

THE COOL AIR was refreshing as it hit my face. Nathan and I were joining some local Hadzabe for an early morning hunt and search for honey. The sun had yet to rise, and a sense of calm filled the day as we waited for activity and movement to begin. I looked around and saw various Hadzabe men grabbing bows and arrows, along with their hatchets and buckets used for collecting honey. Each Hadzabe man held his bow and arrows in the left hand, balanced his hatchet over his shoulder, and tied a small bucket to his back using a blanket called a Shuka.

The gear was packed, the men were ready, and we were soon on our way! Keeping up with Hadzabe on a hunt is quite a task. Their hiking pace is comparable to an athlete speed walking through an airport hoping to make a flight. We found out fast: if you want to keep up, you better move quick!

We hiked up and down several steep hills covered in rocks, passed through dried-up rivers, and strategically avoided bushes full of the biggest thorns I had ever seen in my life. At the top of one hill, one of the Hadzabe hunters, Sigwazi, pulled out a couple of sticks and a wad of dry grass. He arranged the sticks between his hands, rapidly rubbed them together, and sparked a small fire.

Adding a couple of small branches to the pile, the fire was formed and steady.

After a few minutes, Sigwazi pulled one of the lit sticks, snuffed out the flame engulfing it, and carried it to a nearby tree. He stuck the smoldering stick inside the tree stump and began to smoke out the beehive inside. When the smoke had done its work, he reached his hand inside the tree and pulled out a honeycomb nearly a foot in diameter. Success! Sigwazi avoided multitudes of smoked-out bees with the small price of a few stings. Holding the honeycomb between his hands as if it were a sandwich, Sigwazi chomped down on his harvested feast, larvae and all.

Wanting us to join him in the celebration, Sigwazi broke off a few pieces of the honeycomb and handed them to us. I took a large bite. The honeycomb was incredibly delicious, full of rich honey with a nice crunch. I enjoyed every bite—that is, until I bit into a cell full of larvae. If you've ever enjoyed the tasty goodness of a Fruit Gusher soft candy, you'll know what I'm about to explain. The larvae exploded and sent their "flavor" darting into every millimeter of my mouth—every tooth crevice, every gum lining, every space in and around my tongue. It was a sour milk taste like none other I've tasted. It's safe to say that was my last piece of larva for the day!

At another tree, Sigwazi looked over and said to me, "Why don't *you* pull out this honeycomb?"

"I'm not sure," I hesitantly replied. "What about all these bees? I've never been stung by an African bee before."

Sigwazi smiled and urged me to give it a try. "Don't worry," he said with confidence, "these are not the large bees you saw before. The small bees live in this tree and they don't sting."

I took a deep breath, reached my hand in the tree, and pulled out a piece of honeycomb. What a thrilling experience! Following the same munching routine of the first round of honey (larva bites aside), we all enjoyed a second helping of honey. And the honey from this comb was even sweeter than the first.

"How many different kinds of honey do you normally collect?" I inquired, desiring to try them all.

"There are about three or four types from the different bees," Sigwazi replied. "We have already tasted honey from the large bees and small bees in the trees. We can also try flower honey."

We continued our journey and found ourselves looking up at a towering baobab tree. It was wider than the length of a car! Every time I see these trees, I wonder, *Who was here when this tree first began to grow? Who walked this ground? Some of these trees were likely around in the day of Jesus!*

One of the men, Sipiti, chopped off a branch from a nearby bush, cut it into eight-inch lengths, and began sharpening the sections into spikes. Spikes sharpened and ready, Sipiti gripped his hatchet, turned it backward, and began effortlessly hammering the spikes into the center of the baobab tree one by one. As he set each spike, he continued to ascend the tree swiftly, fearlessly, and with precision. Near the top of the tree, Sipiti sauntered out on one of the branches. Fully defying gravity and the fear of falling, he leaned way out and grabbed a baobab fruit.

Sipiti moved on to the next task. Returning to the trunk, he climbed higher. "There is a good amount of rain water here!" he declared. Sipiti lowered the bucket he was carrying into the trunk, filled it with water, and swiftly returned to the ground as speedily as he had ascended. I was once again amazed how the Hadzabe use every resource available to them. The men passed the bucket around and drank from it. I also slurped out some water through my LifeStraw filter. These few gulps provided the sustenance necessary to continue the hunt that was far from over!

With typical Hadzabe pace, we continued the hunt—our focus now on animals. As our hunting party came to the top of a ridge, my heart pounded with excitement as we watched an entire herd of zebras scamper over the next hill and down into a valley. Adrenaline pumping, we quickly pursued them. *We could feast tonight!* I thought as we tightened the gap between us and our potential dinner. But as we neared their location, the men stopped.

"What is going on?" I asked. "Why aren't we following the zebras?"

"We cannot go over there," one of the men said.

I was puzzled. "What do you mean we can't go there?" I inquired.

"That place is Dundubi. We cannot go there."

Still confused, I asked, "What is Dundubi? What is wrong with that place?"

"It is a dangerous place," he explained. "There is a special rock there. And when you tap it, the rock makes noises like *ting ting ting, tink tink tink, tong tong tong*." What he described sounded to me like what a metal marimba would produce.

He continued, "To go there, you must bring a village elder and tap on the rock in a particular order. It is also helpful to smoke marijuana once you arrive. Then our ancestor spirits will appear in front of you. Each person must approach them and say, 'We are just here to bless you. Can I enter?' and then the spirit will decide who can enter. And if they give you permission, you may join those who hike up to the top of the rock mountain to pray for rain, provision, and blessing."

"What happens if someone does not do this?" I asked.

"The spirits will be very angry!" he replied. "One time a man went there, and he did not please the spirits. They stripped him of his clothes and he fearfully ran away almost completely naked. Another time, someone became confused and was lost in the bush for three days. We have seen these things happen before." Then, as if to summarize, he said, "It is a very dangerous place!"

I thought for a moment and then responded. "The other night we told you about Jesus, and you all said you wanted to follow Him, right?"

"Yes we did," several of the men affirmed.

"Jesus has power over everything, including these ancestor spirits," I proclaimed. "We do not have to be afraid. You must not pray to these spirits or interact with them anymore. You can go there and the only thing you will say to them is, 'Go away in the name of Jesus!'"

"Let us try to go tomorrow with Onwas, our village elder," they responded.

"Okay," I affirmed. "We will pray today and go tomorrow."

We began our several-hour hike back to the village. When we arrived, we told Onwas about our journey, and he agreed to go to Dundubi with us the next morning. Nathan and I prayed and felt that God certainly wanted us to go to this place of spiritual darkness.

That night, I laid in the tent with pressing anticipation yet strong uncertainty of what we might find at Dundubi. I was not afraid, as I knew that Jesus was with us and would shelter us. I felt confident and expectant that His power would be revealed.

The next morning, we awoke before daylight and began our five-hour journey into the bush. One hour into the hike, we began ascending a rocky hill. Onwas huffed and puffed, clearly struggling to breathe. "I am an old man," he said. "You all go on without me. I cannot make the journey."

Although most of the Hadzabe do not know how old they are, I suspected Onwas to be in his seventies. Onwas turned back toward the village, and we continued onward toward Dundubi.

We eventually reached the same ridge where we had seen zebras the day before. The view was incredible. It overlooked a valley covered with trees and thornbushes that led up to the rock mountain in front of us. Dundubi began somewhere at the base of that mountain. The young men hesitated, then came to a halt. Motionless, no one said a word.

"We cannot go," they declared.

"What do you mean?" I asked. "We have come all this way once again."

"It is too dangerous," they decreed, stricken with paralyzing fear.

"As we told you, Jesus really is more powerful than these spirits," I declared. "If you truly want to follow Him, you will discover that this is true! We can go there and declare the name of Jesus and nothing bad will happen. He will protect us."

Anger rose in their voices. "No! You do not understand! We must not go to Dundubi!" they demanded. "You cannot understand these things!"

Questions and thoughts flooded my mind: *What should we do?*

What could we do? One option would be to venture out to Dundubi on our own. But that might not be the best idea.

Amid the chaos I turned to the one who made Dundubi and all that surrounded it and asked, "God, what do you want us to do?" As these thoughts burned on my heart, God answered, *"Don't worry. I will provide a Joshua or Caleb to take you into the land."*

We journeyed back to camp that afternoon without ever reaching Dundubi. We did not know how or when we would get there, but we knew God would make a way if He really wanted us to go.

That night, as we were finishing up our campfire-cooked dinner, Sigwazi approached Nathan and me and asked to speak with us privately. He said, "I will take you. We will go to Dundubi tomorrow morning."

For the third day in a row, we awoke before daybreak and began the extensive journey toward Dundubi. As the cool of the morning faded to daylight, the scorching sun beat down on us. The next several hours were exhausting, but we arrived at the base of Dundubi once again. We each prayed along these lines: "God, please protect us and arm us with all your armor: the helmet of salvation, the breastplate of righteousness, the belt of truth, the shoes of the gospel of peace, the shield of faith, and the sword of the Spirit. Have your way in this place!" (Ephesians 6:10–20).

After we prayed, we began our ascent, cautiously climbing the red-faced rock at a near forty-five-degree incline. About halfway up the mountain, we came to the special *ting, tink, tong* rock the hunting group told us about a few days prior.

"Incredible," I said, "this rock is unlike anything I have ever seen!" The rock was about the size of a truck and split in two. The outside was red and the inside gray. Something had broken this solid rock in half. Maybe lightning. Or perhaps it was some sort of asteroid that cracked apart upon landing. Whatever it was, it looked incredible! Little divots peppered the face of the rock. I picked up a small stone and began to tap on those divots. Sure enough, the musical *ting, tink, tong* song echoed into the valley. Thoughts flooded my mind of when I was a young boy tapping metal posts at recess. The sound was so unnatural for a rock.

We continued praying as we ventured upward. When we reached the top, I peered over the edge. What a breathtaking view! This cliff overlooked the entirety of the wild bush and the entire region around Lake Eyasi. In a loud voice and with great confidence, I declared, "In the name of Jesus, we command any spirits to flee this place. Go away now! Go wherever Jesus sends you. We claim this land for Jesus and His kingdom cause. Lord, will You change this place and take ahold of the hearts of the Hadzabe people? From now on, we pray that this place be marked by You and no longer by darkness. This mountain has represented the spiritual darkness and bondage that has held back the Hadzabe people from the light of the gospel for generations. Lord God Almighty, from this day forward, may this place be marked by Your light, Your freedom, and Your Kingdom!"

Sigwazi muttered, "I don't understand why nothing bad has happened yet. I was afraid going up. I expected that something bad would definitely happen and that the spirits would attack us."

"We told you, Sigwazi, Jesus is more powerful. He can protect us against the darkness," I assured him. "You must go back and tell everyone in the village what happened and what Jesus did here today."

We looked around and gathered as many large rocks as we could find. We carried them to a visible spot on the incline of the mountain and placed the rocks together in the form of a cross. We wanted anyone traveling near Dundubi to see and know that this place was now marked by Jesus and His power over the darkness. We prayed and poured some oil onto these rocks. We anointed them for the Lord, hopeful that this would become a place known by, above all else, His power. My thoughts turned toward Genesis 35:14 when Jacob anointed a rock pillar after a significant spiritual experience with the Lord in order to remember what God had done and set that place apart for God above all else. We wanted to do the same in Dundubi.

When we returned to the village, we shared what we experienced at Dundubi. Onwas and Mary had been sitting outside our tents awaiting our return. Onwas confidently declared, "I have been praying for you all day. I knew you would return without any problems!"

The young men of the village, however, expressed a different tone and spirit. "No!" they said. "It is not possible. We don't believe you actually went to Dundubi. You still do not understand. You cannot do that!"

Unfortunately, these young men did not have ears to hear what God was saying and doing. They continued living their lives gripped by fear, entrapped by Satan's stronghold. On the other hand, Onwas, Mary, and Sigwazi overcame fear. They discovered the rock-solid reality that Jesus has all authority. And His authority is not limited to this "earth" but extends into the heavenly places and all spiritual realms (Matthew 28:18).

We do not fight against people who come against us; rather, we battle "against the spiritual forces of evil in the heavenly places" (Ephesians 6:12 ESV). And in those heavenly places, Jesus has all authority. That's why we can experience radical shelter . . . here, there, and everywhere!

My family once entered a hotel that had a Buddhist statue in the front lobby. Not that an idol is anything in and of itself, but I do know there are spiritual forces behind them (Deuteronomy 32:16–17; 1 Corinthians 10:19–20). The hotel lobby loomed with a sense of darkness—in the spiritual realm, the "heavenly places."

So as I entered our room, I prayed over it, "Lord, will you protect us here? I command anything not of God to flee this place in Jesus' name. Lord, will You send Your guardian angels to stand at the door so that anything in opposition to You cannot enter? Thank You, God!"

A few minutes later, the lady who had been running the hotel came down the hallway wheeling the rollaway bed we requested. I expected her to do what a typical hotel service member often does in similar situations: bring the bed into the room and ask if anything else might be needed. But that's not what happened. As soon as the lady came within five feet of our door, she stopped in her tracks. A disturbed and fearful look came across her face. Then she blurted out, "Here is the bed," as she quickly did an about-face and retreated down the hallway.

"Praise You, Lord!" I prayed, "You really are serious about protecting us here!"

When we engage places and people who reside in the kingdom of darkness, we have radical shelter. When the kingdom of darkness sends messengers to attack us, we have radical shelter. And when we infiltrate regions still ruled by the kingdom of darkness and gripped by Satan for generations, even there we have radical shelter.

Have you experienced God's radical shelter in the midst of darkness? We are at war. Arrows are flying. Danger is near. Fear might be rising. But I tell you, it's time! Proclaim the name of Jesus out loud! Lift up the shield of faith! Extinguish the fiery arrows of the enemy!

Now What?

- Read 1 John 5:19. How have you seen the kingdom of darkness at work in our fallen world?
- How is the spiritual battle waging war against you personally?
- Next time the darkness comes against you, how will you take up the radical shelter that Jesus (the one with *all* authority) offers you?

TWENTY-SEVEN
WARFARE

"I HAVE NO PEACE. Something is not right," Mary shared.

Ever since Mary decided to follow Jesus, we have known her to be a woman marked by abiding peace. She has a calming disposition—one of love, contentment, goodness . . . peace. So we knew something must be really off when she said, "I do not have peace."

"Okay, Mary, we should pray together and seek Jesus about this," I said. "When would you like to pray together?"

"Let's see how the day goes and pray together this evening," she replied.

"Okay. That sounds good," I agreed. "Meanwhile, Nathan and I will be praying for you throughout the day."

We finished breakfast and began our day. Our next task for the day was a training session with twelve Hadzabe people who had come to know Jesus. We were meeting together twice daily, once in the morning and once at night. We took a break during the day so that those being trained to be "fishers of men" could also be hunters and gatherers of food.

A few minutes after our morning teaching ended, some of the villagers ecstatically jumped to their feet and pointed toward a spot on the mountain behind our camp. Halfway up the slope was a group of forty or so baboons running across the mountain terrain. They were jumping around and dodging rocks as they scampered along the way.

I yelled to Onwas, "*Ning-ay-penda Nay-eh-nay sana!*" (translated, "I really want baboon."). "We need to hunt some!"

Onwas laughed, air drafting to the back of his mouth as he shook his head side to side. "Oh, Shakwa," he said, "we will get one for you sometime." Shakwa is the Hadzabe name that Onwas gave me during my second trip to their people. It means "short bush tree" (okay, just stop your laughing, all right! I get it, I'm not the tallest guy on the block). The baboons were gone from our sight nearly as quickly as they entered. I would have to take Onwas's promise of bagging a baboon "sometime" on another day.

After our evening training, Nathan and I met Mary around our campfire just outside our tent. "I still have no peace in my heart, and I don't know why," Mary said.

"That's okay, sister," we encouraged her. "Although we have no idea why you are lacking peace, Jesus knows. Let's ask Jesus about your lack of peace and see if He brings anything to mind."

"Let's try that," Mary affirmed.

Bowing our heads, we sought the Prince of Peace. "Jesus, you know Mary has no peace today. We don't know why. Will you help us? Will you speak to us? What's causing this?"

Our words ceased, and we sat in silence for a few minutes—waiting and listening for the Lord to bring clarity to this situation as He saw fit. All of a sudden, Mary said, "I know why! This just came to me: this is an attack of the devil! The devil does not want me to translate the Word of God, because he doesn't want these people to know more about who Jesus is."

"We must rebuke him now!" I exclaimed.

"Yes, definitely!" Mary replied.

"In the name of Jesus we rebuke the attack of the enemy," I declared in prayer. "Any spirits that are coming against the work of God here, we command you to leave. Go away in the name of Jesus! And Lord, would You fill Mary with your Spirit, fully empowering her for all that You have called her to? Would You fill

her with Your peace that is so much greater than any understanding?"

A smile widened on Mary's face, "I am completely at peace
again!" she proclaimed.

"Praise You, Lord Jesus! You are so good!" Nathan shouted.

Have you ever watched *National Geographic* or some other
adventure show where a lion prowls silently through the grass
toward an absolutely absentminded, grass-eating gazelle? Eventually, the hidden lion lunges into the open, pounces on its prey,
shredding and devouring it. No more gazelle.

That is exactly what is happening in the unseen spiritual realm
right now. The Bible tells us that our enemy, the devil, prowls
around like a roaring lion seeking someone to devour (1 Peter
5:8). He wants to tear you to pieces just like that gazelle. These
aren't just flowery words or hyperbole. This is not simply an
ancient, unscientific way to understand reality. The spiritual battle
is real. And if you have not realized that, you might be wandering
around like an absentminded gazelle.

The spiritual battle must be engaged for us to effectively run
the race and advance God's kingdom. "For our struggle is not
against flesh and blood, but against . . . the spiritual forces of evil
in the heavenly realms" (Ephesians 6:12 NIV). This is exactly what
came against Mary. The spiritual forces of evil hate those who
commit to the cause of Christ and even wage war against them
(Revelation 12:17). So if you seek to obey Jesus and advance His
kingdom, I have news for you. Satan hates your guts and is actively
waging war against you!

The spiritual realm continually amazes and surprises me. I
certainly do not have it all figured out. It's quite mysterious. And
at times, I still think it's all a bit crazy. But what I do know is that
as I have engaged God's mission, I have experienced spiritual
opposition. While it is often difficult to comprehend the fullness
of the spiritual battle all around us and the satanic attacks we may
face as believers, I have discovered and come to know with absolute confidence that Jesus is all powerful.

Too often in our day, we ignore the spiritual realm and undermine its reality. We live spiritually unaware—like absentminded gazelles, oblivious to what is happening. The Scriptures offer an alternative way: be sober minded and watchful (1 Peter 5:8) by effectively using the weapons that have been given to us to overcome our enemy.

Equally, we must be cautious not to swing the pendulum too far by overemphasizing the attacks of the enemy, thus causing unnecessary and ungodly fear. Although I probably looked like a frightful gazelle that one time I ran from a lion, we need not flee in fear when it comes to our prowling enemy, the devil. Rather, we can stand firm because of Jesus! With Him we are victorious!

So how do we engage this battle? Throughout the Gospels and the book of Acts we see the power and authority that comes with the name of Jesus. When the enemy attacks, we must proclaim Jesus' name out loud! Mary victoriously wrestled against the darkness as she confidently declared the name of Jesus.

While I have seen times of victory in the battle, I'm not a spiritual warfare superstar. Quite the contrary. There have been plenty of occasions I have felt inadequate for the task and clueless about what to do. One such occasion was a time I was walking through the woods in the middle of the night.

I am not typically afraid of the dark, but this time was different. I was leading a discipleship training event with a group of young people, and I think the enemy hated how many of them were being transformed by Jesus. As I walked through the woods, I was stricken with fear from head to toe. It was some of the deepest fear I ever remember facing. My body was trembling. All around me, the air felt chaotic. It was the kind of fear that can paralyze you in your tracks.

In many ways I had no idea what to do, how to get beyond the fear. The only thing that came to me was the one thing I needed most: begin praising Jesus! So I began to praise Him and sing His name out loud. Anyone who sits near me in church can tell you—I am anything but a good singer! I didn't care. God wasn't after my voice; He wanted my heart. So I sang and praised out loud! And as I did, the most incredible thing happened: the spiritual darkness that was hovering over me disappeared . . . and I was filled with peace.

Experiencing demonic fear? Praise and proclaim Jesus out loud and proud! Don't be shy! I guarantee you, your singing voice is better than mine.

There's power in praise. There's also great power in God's Word. God instructs us to take up the "sword of the Spirit, which is the word of God" (Ephesians 6:17 NIV). My wife once joined me for a venture into the bush. One night she was suddenly struck with abdominal pain. The pain became so extreme that she couldn't sleep. All she could do was clench her stomach and moan.

I laid next to her in the tent wondering what in the world I could do to help her. I mean we were out in the middle of nowhere! I decided to pray quietly, "Lord, what should I do?" Immediately, His Spirit brought these words to mind: *"Read the Bible out loud."* So I opened my Bible and began reading out loud from the book of Psalms. I kept reading well into the night, psalm after psalm, until my wife was able to fall asleep.

The next morning she shared with me, "Every time you read the Word of God out loud, my pain decreased from what felt like level 10 to a level 2."

I was amazed. God's Word proclaimed by the Spirit's leading shined light into darkness, and the darkness fled. I cannot fully explain how or why this works. But I know that Jesus Himself quoted Scripture out loud to fight Satan (Luke 4:1–13). There is power in His Word! It's time for more of us to seriously grip a hold of the sword of the Spirit and start kicking some demon butt!

Do not forget, the battle is real. There is an unseen realm that seeks to wage war against those of us who are obeying Jesus and running the race! Don't be surprised by the spiritual battle all around. When trouble comes, ask God to give you eyes to see, stand firm, and, with the sword of the Spirit in hand, wage war.

Finally, be watchful but not afraid. Submit to God, resist the devil, and he will flee from you (James 4:7). It is not overly complicated: proclaim His name out loud, praise Him, and wield His Word! God will be with you!

Now What?

- Can you think of a time when you engaged the spiritual battle through saying the name of Jesus out loud, praising God, or quoting Scripture out loud?
- Read Ephesians 4:26–27. Are there some ways you have stopped resisting and therefore begun to let the enemy gain strongholds in your life? What are they? Prayerfully repent of them: give them over to Jesus asking for His forgiveness and for power to walk in His resurrection victory in these areas of your life!
- Jesus quoted memorized Scripture to successfully fight the spiritual battle. It's time to commit His Word to memory. What Scriptures can you begin to memorize right now?

TWENTY-EIGHT

RESISTANCE

"GOD, do you really want me to go here? If you do, why does the door to going seem to be closed shut?!"

I had applied for a visa to somewhere in South Asia. I got denied. I had no idea why; the rejection letter never said. I had no idea what to do, so I continued praying. I wondered if I simply needed to trash the whole idea of the trip. Was there really any other option?

That night, I opened my Bible and was stunned by what I read: "We wanted to come to you—I, Paul, again and again—but Satan hindered us" (1 Thessalonians 2:18 ESV). Paul's experience was my reality, but I hadn't realized it. At that point I had not yet considered that Satan might stop me from going.

I cannot tell you how many times I've heard people proclaim with God-like confidence, "Well, the Lord must be closing the door to that country. It's probably better you stay home anyway." But let's be honest. No matter how well intended, what that statement really conveys is, "God doesn't want us to go make disciples in that place. We should go somewhere safer and easier anyway." What a boatload of lies! Of course God wants us to go to *all* nations, no matter the cost!

As I opened my Bible to 1 Thessalonians 2:18, the truth had been revealed: a seemingly "closed door" may not be God's leading but rather Satan's resistance! I laid in bed praying and pondering, *What if God really is leading me to go but Satan is hindering me? How would I even work this out?*

I awoke the next morning eager to revisit the scripture I had read the night before. Oddly, I couldn't remember where the passage was found. So I pulled up the web browser on my computer and searched "Satan hindered us." One of the first links on my screen was a sermon titled "Satanic Hindrances" by Charles Spurgeon. I decided to read it and see what God might want to teach me through this renowned preacher.

In his sermon Spurgeon discussed various ways Satan could have hindered Paul and the gang from going to Thessalonica. Whatever it was, one critical spiritual reality must be understood: Satan "was afraid lest the firebrands of gospel truth should be again flung in among the masses, and a gracious [wildfire] should take place." That was my answer! God surely must be calling me to go!

At that time, I was studying in a post-college apprenticeship for itinerant preaching and ministry. The name of the training program: Forge Firebrands. You can imagine what welled up within me as I read these words of Spurgeon. For me there was only one conclusion: God must be calling me to go! I had scarcely heard the word "firebrand" outside of my training program. This holy "coincidence" was no accident or fluke—especially in the context of gospel proclamation!

As my wife and I continued to pray, we were both convinced I must go on this trip. But how?

I can't totally reveal my secret (it would put future trips like this in jeopardy), but I can tell you this: with a little perseverance I did some God-inspired research that resulted in God making a way for me to apply for another visa. And because God was in it—it worked! Visa granted, I would soon be on my way to South Asia.

I can't help but ask, how often does our culture inform our

theology rather than the reverse? While the kingdom cause demands long-suffering perseverance, we live in a fast-food culture in America. Not only do we especially like our food fast, but we like lightning-speed internet, quick cars, short wait times, immediate answers, and Johnny-on-the-spot results for anything we desire. Now, I must confess, I do love fast food (particularly Chick-Fil-A or Chipotle, for those of you familiar with those restaurants). I am often busy running to and fro, doing this, that, and the other so that I don't have the patience to spend time cooking. Praise God for a gracious wife who balances me out!

What happens when this fast-food mentality infiltrates our method of mission? I wonder how often we give up on a God-given direction because it doesn't come quickly or easily enough. Without immediate results we begin to view resistance as a completely "closed door" from God.

I often hear people use the language of "open" and "closed" doors to discern God's will. For example, "This door [i.e., opportunity] has been closed, so God must not want me to go there or do that" or "I am just waiting for an open door" or "This door has been opened, so it must be God's direction for my life." But I am not convinced this is the best way to discern God's direction.

What if there were multiple "open doors" to choose from— then what do we decide? I mean, they can't all be from God. Or what if there are no apparent "open doors"? Then what on Earth do we do? There must be a better way than this. What if Satan is the one who sometimes causes "closed doors," but God wants us to go and knock those doors down anyway? I often wonder if we use the language of a "closed door" as an excuse to back down from difficulty. If we let "open" and "closed" doors lead us, we might be missing out on the fullness of what God has for us, and we may never reach the lost of the world.

I have frequently grappled with the resistance I've seen all over the globe. While attempting to engage unreached people groups, I have encountered landslides blocking the only road in or out, required police escorts, rumors of rebel attacks, government leaders working to shut down our activities, debilitating sicknesses, discouraging and divisive spiritual attacks, fear of danger, fear of the unknown, news of problems back home, vehicle breakdowns, opposition to the mission coming from the very people I would expect to support the mission, not to mention countless other resistances. I have often felt the reality of the words "Satan hindered us." But this should not be a surprise. This should become our expectation.

Satan has kept individuals and entire people groups in bondage for generation after generation. Of course there will be resistance. He has blinded the minds of all unbelievers so they cannot see the light of the gospel (2 Corinthians 4:4). Do you really think that Satan's cool with us prancing in and stirring up his demonic hornet's nest? Do you think he enjoys us piercing his darkness with light? Of course not! Satan wants to seal shut as many doors as he can.

While this is true, the spiritual reality is too often downplayed by statements like "Sure, Satan is 'real,' but let's not give him too much power or recognition by talking too much about him. He doesn't do anything too significant in the world anyway, since God is more powerful." I have two things to say about that. First, I'm not sure how our conversation about spiritual warfare is going to magically empower Satan. He's already ransacking this world (Ephesians 2:1–2; Revelation 2:13). Second, go proclaim Jesus among the unreached and see what happens. I dare you. While you may not travel halfway around the globe, it's likely you could find someone unreached, from an ethnic people group with little to no believers, living as a refugee in your city or a city near you. I imagine you'll discover the enemy's strongholds in the world are far from insignificant. Too many of us need to seriously reread our Bibles.

If God calls you to go and engage an unreached region of the world with absolutely zero believers, it will be difficult. You won't receive a phone call and invitation from them that says, "Please, come join us! We'll be sure to open the door for you." In a lost, dying, and dark world, Jesus' mission will not come to us like a Chick-Fil-A fast-food server bringing a chicken sandwich to our table with a "Would you like any sauces with that? . . . My pleasure."

Whether you're engaging an unreached people group halfway around the globe or your neighbor who is still lost in their sin, don't expect it to be as easy as a simple stroll in the park. When God says, "Go," and you begin running in the direction He points you, the enemy will start slinging demonic mud at you. Even more, Satan will water down your muddy trail and set up every kind of obstacle so that you slow down, slip up, and slink right on back home.

Plain and simple: you will face resistance. That might not be fun to hear, but God has a purpose as we encounter resistance: it makes us stronger. True mudrunners know the value of resistance training. Our physical muscles need resistance to gain strength. No pain, no gain. Why should we expect our spiritual lives to work any differently? Our spiritual muscles also require resistance to grow. Resistance creates opportunity for our own good—and God allows us to encounter it along the way so that we grow in maturity and strength in our faith. Resistance brings God's fullness into our lives (James 1:2–4).

We need the Spirit of God to give us a fresh dose of perseverance and long-suffering once again! Let's ask Him for that. Let's run this race with endurance by the mighty power of God! Let's sprint hard for His kingdom, no matter how many "closed doors" we face! It's time to "embrace the suck" of the resistance with pure joy and knock down some doors in the name of Jesus (spiritually speaking, of course!).

Now What?

- Have you ever considered that Satan could potentially cause a "closed door"? What do you think about this reality?

- When spiritual resistance or difficulty comes your way, do you embrace it or run from it? How so?
- For the sake of your spiritual growth and the advancement of God's kingdom, how will you practically engage trials and resistance going forward?

TWENTY-NINE

THE HUMBLE EXALTED

MARY HAD BEEN at the market and begun her walk home. It was an ordinary African afternoon—including the intense heat radiating from the sun. The events that were about to happen next, however, were anything but ordinary. And they would turn her family's world upside down.

When Mary arrived home, the front door was locked. She set down the groceries she was carrying and walked around to the side of her mud-brick hut. Peering inside the window, she gasped. Everything was gone. She hadn't been burglarized. There had been no thief. No, it was worse. Mary's husband sold everything they had—including the house—and disappeared, never to return again. Mary was devastated. She was left with absolutely nothing.

That night, Mary and her two young children slept outside on the dirt. They shared the cover of a thin blanket that somehow escaped her husband's betrayal. As the night got colder, Mary and the kids scooted together to maximize their body heat and squelch their shivering.

Day after day, Mary was left destitute and hopeless. The very people that Mary once considered friends turned their backs on her. They actually spit in her face and mocked her. "Look at this woman," they taunted. "She is nothing now!"

Eventually Mary turned to alcohol to soothe her pain and fill the void that her husband's leaving handed her. She began visiting the village bar. With her pain temporarily drowned for the day, Mary would leave the bar and aimlessly wander through the town. Her repeated routine earned her the title of town drunk. Mary would have never predicted that one sunny afternoon on the way home from the market she'd end up "here." People seldom do.

Mary knew something was still missing in her life. The life she was looking for seemed elusive. Regardless of what she tried, nothing was bringing the hope she desperately desired—and alcohol was only complicating her pursuit.

But that all changed when Mary joined us around a campfire one night, and she decided to follow Jesus. The extreme difficulty and sheer hopelessness Mary faced made the Holy Spirit's first words to her all the more profound: *"Do not be afraid of the diffi-culty. I will be with you."* I immediately knew these were God's words to Mary—the same words God often spoke to His people all throughout Scripture!

God's words entered Mary's heart and met her at her greatest place of need. Mary understood God's message to her: *"When others reject you, Mary, I will be with you. When difficulties stare you in the face, Mary, I will uphold you."*

That evening around the campfire, Mary focused her eyes on Jesus and never looked back. She began experiencing the peace that Jesus offers, the peace that surpasses our understanding. And as she continued to abide in Christ and sit in the heavenly realms with Him, Mary launched an amazing ministry to her people. She began regularly proclaiming the good news of Jesus Christ to the lost in various villages and initiated (along with others) a local house church gathering. Mary became a mudrunner.

Today Mary continues to put love in action as Hadzabe tribals come from all over the bush and stay in her home. If they are passing through to another village, her home is *the* layover point.

In fact, ten to fifteen people might be staying at her home at any given time. God has given Mary a love without limits.

Amazingly, the people who once mocked Mary are the very ones now coming to her for food, for their survival. "Mary, please feed us. We are starving."

And while these formerly proud mockers have come to fill their bellies, they have begun to discover sustenance for their souls. Not only does Mary house and feed anyone in need, she also shares the bread that truly lasts—the bread of life. Everyone in the region knows who Mary is. As Mary has continued to follow Jesus faithfully and use her influence to help others as she brings glory to God, it's not a stretch to say, Mary has become famous among her people. She has even become a sought-after leader, giving counsel among her entire tribe as well as among other tribes seeking to interact with the Hadzabe.

Mary's life reminds me of Joseph from the Scriptures. Joseph was ridiculed, thrown into a pit, and sold into slavery by his own brothers. However, after his humble beginnings and a journey chock-full of difficulty and suffering, Joseph's fame spread as his influence grew. The same brothers who once mocked Joseph came bowing down to him and seeking his help for their survival (Genesis 37–42).

Just like God brought Joseph out of a pit and into a place of influence, God took Mary—a brokenhearted, rejected, drunken homeless woman—helped her up from the dirt, gave her a place to stand, and provided her purpose and direction. From mud puddle to mudrunner, Mary has become a respected woman of influence among her people.

Could it be God wants to do the same for you? God is in the business of lifting up the lowly while simultaneously fighting against the proud (Proverbs 29:23; Matthew 23:12; Luke 1:52; Luke 14:10; James 4:6, 10).

Mary knows and embraces the power of humility. She has never been too high-and-mighty to get on her knees, roll up her sleeves, and engage the mud puddles of human need.

One day while we were sitting in our bush camp, Mary reflected back on her life and all that God had done: "You know, you are like John the Baptist in my life. You were the key that God used to open my life to Jesus. Now everything is different."

Mary was kind to make that comparison. I pray God continues to use us in that way for His kingdom's sake and glory. As Mary pointed us to John—a fiery-eyed, wild-man prophet—my mind was drawn to his bold proclamation: "He must increase, but I must decrease" (John 3:30 ESV). Essentially, John was proclaiming, "Jesus must be great, not me!" I love how David Eubank's film *Free Burma Rangers* puts it: "Be bold in the things of Jesus, but be humble in the things of yourself."[1]

What if you lived a life of humility? What if your life was marked by a continual expression of "Jesus must be greater, I must be less"? I imagine you would see God working in new and fresh ways. I imagine there would be incredible opportunity for kingdom impact. I envision the legacy of your life "preparing the way of the Lord" for many. That's what John the Baptist did in his day. It wasn't about him. It was all about Jesus coming and transforming hearts and lives. God can use you to do the same.

Only after Jesus humbled himself to death on a cross was He resurrected and exalted to the highest place. We, too, must humble ourselves. God's promise is clear: the humble will be exalted. Equally comes His warning: the exalted will be humbled.

So, will you seek to serve or be served? Will you roll up your sleeves to engage the dirty mud puddles of human need, or will you remain primarily focused on *your* needs, wants, and plans?

Now What?

- Read Philippians 2:3–9. Is your life marked more by humility (considering others as more important than yourself) or pride (looking out for your own interests first and foremost)? How so?
- How can you become less and Jesus become greater in your life?

- What would it look like for you to choose humility this week?

THIRTY

RADICAL SUBMISSION

"IS this really the wisest thing to do?"

"You know this is a massive decision. Can you really decide this quickly?"

"Maybe you should wait until after military school before deciding to go this new direction."

It was time. I had reached a fork in the road. A radically life-changing decision stared me in the face. There were many voices and opinions, but the ultimate choice was mine alone. This one decision would alter the entire direction of the rest of my life.

It's crazy to think that the impact of a single moment can be so far-reaching that one of our finite minutes in time can really matter that much. We don't always expect such moments, nor do we always know their significance at the time. For me, one moment, of one message, through one man, changed everything!

Most of us have life goals and dreams. I desired to attend the United States Air Force Academy or West Point and become a fighter pilot or Special Forces officer. From seventh grade through my senior year of high school, I worked hard to reach my goal and obtain my dream. Everything I did pointed toward this vision. I took advanced classes, served as a wrestling team captain, ran cross-country, became a sergeant with Police Explorers, started a summer landscaping company, joined the worship leadership team for our youth ministry, engaged in youth group every week, and volunteered as a youth leader for junior high students. And that list contains only the highlights! Let's just say, my eyes were set on a successful military career, and I was going to do anything necessary to get there!

I was so laser focused on *my* dream that my parents wanted to make sure I was seeing all sides and angles of my life. They loved me and didn't want me to get blindsided. And while they were super supportive (and extremely proud) of my decision to serve our country in such a way, they wanted God's best for me most of all—whether that meant the military or another vocation.

I recall my mom occasionally checking in with me about my dream. She wanted to make sure this was the right direction for my life. About the third or fourth time she asked me, "Are you sure you want to commit your entire career to the military?" my seventeen-year-old self was sure it was the fortieth time.

In anger I arrogantly replied, "Yes! This is what I'm doing. I'm joining the military and making a career out of it. So stop asking me!"

I was immovable. Nothing and no one could stop me. The vice president of the United States as well as a state senator nominated me for both the Air Force Academy and West Point. The military offered me full-ride Air Force and Army ROTC scholarships to engineering schools. I had embraced a military future.

In fact, I had officially taken the oath to defend the Constitution and was simply waiting with great anticipation for my military schooling to begin. My military career was so close to launch time, and my dream was in my hands!

Before departing for military training, my church's youth pastor called me. "Hey, Charlie, are you interested in joining me for a five-day summer camp? I would love for you to come with me and help me see if the camp might be a good fit for our youth group."

"Sure!" I told him. "I'd love to go. I'll take a week off my landscaping job and join you." The thought of one last hoorah at a camp in the Rocky Mountains for a week sounded pretty good before I hit the high demands of military life. Little did I know, God had a few surprises up His sleeve!

I entered the camp thinking, *I know what I need to know and have a solid grasp on most things.* And I did, in fact, know my Bible left and right. But what I didn't realize was that my life looked more like the Pharisees than Jesus. That week, the preaching struck my heart unlike anything I had ever experienced. For some reason, this time was different.

I sat on the edge of my seat, enthralled in a message about proclaiming the gospel in dark, dangerous, and despised places around the globe. The preacher talked about disciple-making movements among the unreached and how it all began for him as he listened to God's prompting, saying yes to Jesus—no matter the people, the place, or the cost. I was hooked by his message. Hooked because it was God's message to me. And when the invitation came, it changed everything. It was the spark that lit a wildfire in my heart and life.

This preacher invited us to prayerfully ask God if He had anything to say to us or any next steps to give us. He instructed us to ask God this question and then simply listen. I had never prayed in such a way before. For some reason, I never realized the Spirit of God could lead us with such clarity.

So I prayed as the preacher instructed. "God," I said, "I'm not sure about this message. I don't know what I think about it. It even seems kind of weird. But if you have anything to say to me, I will listen." In that very moment, an image popped into my imagination: I saw a grassy field in darkness. Then a bright light flashed, and fire suddenly passed through the field.

What was that? I thought. *That was crazy! I saw that picture in my imagination, but it certainly didn't originate with me. It was something totally different. This must be from the Lord. I wonder what God is trying to show me?* God had just lit a match to set my spiritual life on fire . . . and I didn't even know it yet.

That same week, as I was spending time with God in prayer,

God continued the conversation: *"Charlie, you are willing to risk your life for your country. Are you willing to do that for Me?"*

God was calling me to more, but what did that "more" look like? Whatever it might look like, I was ready to commit to Jesus in doing it. One week later, I found myself hitting my knees at the foot of a large cross in an open field.

As I prayed, once again God began to speak—this time more clearly than ever before: *"Charlie, Will you surrender the military and put me first in your life?"*

God's question penetrated the deepest regions of my soul. His words—powerful and fresh, exciting and compelling, mysterious and peace filled—had me on my knees with my white flag raised. I was ready to give up doing life on *my* terms.

Yes, Lord, I prayed. *I surrender and put You first in my life.*

I felt the Lord continue: *"If you mean it, then get on your face before Me."*

But Lord, I protested, *there are all sorts of ants and dirt here, and I don't want to look like one of those freak Christians either.*

Again, God's words came to me: *"If you mean it, then get on your face before Me."*

So I laid flat on my face and declared my all-in allegiance: *God, whatever you want to do with my life, do it. I am willing. Lord, I submit to You. Whatever You have for my life, I'm all in.*

This moment—the "on my face in prayer at the foot of the cross" moment—became the spiritual tipping point of my life. There was no turning back. My life would never be the same. I was all in for Jesus—no matter what was ahead, no matter what it might cost me.

The pivotal, turning-point moment behind me came with a new set of questions: *What now, Lord? What's next? How do You want me to serve You?* I had no idea what to do. I had already taken the oath to defend the Constitution. I had committed myself to a military career. I had no alternate vision of what to do with my life. All my eggs were in one basket.

While I didn't know the next step for my life, I knew God did.

So that week I grabbed my Bible and went to the woods to spend time with God and seek His direction.

I prayed, *God, I have no idea what to do. I am surrendered to You, whatever that looks like. But unless You show me what to do, I will continue forward with the Air Force yet putting You first.*

As I prayed, Romans 1 burned in my mind. I knew I had to read it. I grabbed my Bible, flipped to the book of Romans, and began reading. As I read, these words jumped off the page as if they were personally meant for me: "called . . . set apart for the gospel . . . to call people from among all the Gentiles to the obedience that comes from faith. . . . God whom I serve with my whole heart in preaching the gospel of his Son is my witness . . . I am obligated both to Greeks and non-Greeks, both to the wise and the foolish. That is why I am so eager to preach the gospel" (Romans 1:1, 5, 9, 14–15 NIV84).

God was calling me into a kingdom purpose that looked similar to the apostle Paul's. I immediately knew what God intended for me: to itinerantly preach. God was calling me to travel, like Paul, from place to place and preach to those who know Jesus but could grow deeper in their passion for Him. Equally, God was calling me to proclaim the gospel to those who have yet to know Him, even venturing into unreached, dangerous places around the world to do so. The picture/vision of the dark field overcome by fire and light God had revealed to me at the summer camp began to make sense: God wanted me to take His light to dark places and spark spiritual fires!

I had a choice to make. Would I obediently submit to Jesus no matter what it cost me, or would I resist? Would I immediately do what He asked, or would I delay my obedience for options that were more logical, comfortable, people pleasing, and safe?

I knew what I had to do. I quit my landscaping job and took the appropriate steps to back out of my military scholarship and schooling. Throughout the whole process, I kept praying, *Lord, I trust You will provide. I have saved zero dollars for college because the military was going to cover everything. I don't believe I should have debt for what You are calling me to do. I trust You are able to provide all I need.*

The same week I exited the military, I applied for a Bible college. I submitted my application on Friday and school started on Monday (crazy, right?!). Amazingly, I was accepted and given various scholarships. Several ministry and internship opportunities became available. And God provided! Miraculously, I graduated college debt-free. Through prayer, hard work, and the gracious outpouring of kingdom resources by other believers, God made a way!

Everything I've witnessed God do began with that single moment of submission—that moment where I acknowledged Jesus was in charge and I was not. The statement "Jesus is Lord" means Jesus holds all authority. Naturally, authority requires submission. Even more, *radical* authority requires *radical* submission, and I would venture to say that Jesus has radical authority. Our only response should be radical submission.

I gave Jesus my all-in "yes" when I hit that fork-in-the-road moment praying before a cross. And I've never looked back. That single moment altered the entire course of my life, and not a day goes by that I regret it.

But that "yes" was only the beginning of a daily journey of radical submission to Jesus. Despite all the unknowns, difficulties, and barriers along the way, radical "yesses" to Jesus have been, by far, worth it! This Jesus adventure is the most fulfilling cause anyone could ever join. I have discovered that Jesus satisfies more than the American dream or any other dream anyone comes up with. In fact, the most elaborate and outlandish dream we could ever conceive of, create, or contrive falls woefully short compared to His kingdom cause. The American dream really is a lame waste of your life. And *our* own individual dreams, if they are not God's also, leave us hollow and empty 100 percent of the time. In fact, they are far too small compared to His kingdom cause, across the street and around the globe! Don't waste your life. After all, your finite minutes matter. Giving God radical control of your life isn't always easy . . . but participating in *His* kingdom dream brings joy beyond your wildest imagination!

Have you given everything for the cause that counts? Have you laid down *your* dreams and asked God for *His* dreams? You won't regret it. Radical submission to the King of Kings is where all true mudrunners must begin their race. Will you commit to saying yes to Jesus no matter the cost and begin taking small steps of obedience today?

Now What?

- Prayerfully consider, what are some things that have crept into your life, and are fighting against your radical submission, therefore taking your full devotion from Jesus and putting more attention on yourself?
- Will you lay down those things that are fighting against your devotion to Jesus and give Him everything? Whether you have never had an absolute surrender moment to Jesus, or you did in the past but a few things have started to divert your devotion, now is the time to pray and tell Jesus, *Lord, I lay myself down and give You everything!*
- What would it look like for you to radically submit to Jesus daily? What can you do to start this week?

THIRTY-ONE

CHOSEN FOR MISSION

AS WE DROVE through desolate desert lands of the East African bush, our team hadn't seen a single person or village for hours. We were literally in the middle of nowhere. Compliments of our uncovered Land Cruiser, dust plastered us from head to toe and stuck to our sweat like sand on peanut butter. After hours of jarring, bump-after-bump off-roading, a tower of giraffes appeared ahead of us in an open valley. And no, the giraffes weren't stacked on top of each other, teetering around like the Leaning Tower of Pisa. A group of giraffes is called a tower (if, like me, you didn't know that fun fact . . . well, now you do!).

As we approached the giraffes, our African friend, Peter, said, "Charlie, why don't you get out and chase them?"

"Are you serious?!" I asked, wondering if he was just egging me on.

"Yes, why not?" Peter smiled.

He didn't need to ask twice. I hopped over the side of the Land Cruiser and into the powdery dust. Peter joined me. We shuffled cautiously toward the giraffes. Nearing the tower, we picked up our pace and accelerated to a full-on sprint toward these magnificent animals. I had no clue if giraffes were ever aggressive toward humans, but if they were, we were certainly done for.

The giraffes scurried in all different directions. Watching giraffes run is amazing! They actually run at high speeds, but their long legs, necks, and stride give the appearance they're running in slow motion. They aren't! Their log-length necks lunging forward through the air, the giraffes outran us. Peter and I bent over to catch our breath, joyously laughing together as we marveled at God's creation.

We climbed back into the vehicle and continued our journey. Just before nightfall, we finally saw signs of human life. It was a Maasai village. Just as we rolled up and put the Land Cruiser in park, several children greeted us. The children were playful and curious. They were especially intrigued with our skin and motioned if they could touch it. We appreciated their sense of wonder and gladly let them. The adults in the village soon approached us and welcomed us to join them.

Someone from our team announced, "We have come to share an important message with you."

The chief replied, "We will kill a goat for everyone and eat. Then you can share your message with us. You are welcome to stay the night in our village too."

Several young warriors brought out a goat to be butchered and cooked. The chief looked at us and said, "One of you can take the honor of slitting its throat and spilling its blood."

No one from our team seemed excited to do the honor. Loving adventure and anything new, I stepped forward and grabbed the machete. With a single swing, our gourmet bush dinner had begun.

The Maasai villagers are good stewards of their resources. After slicing the goat into small pieces, they harvested nearly every piece of the goat. They poked sticks into the sand around the fire and stretched out large portions of meat on them. They also roasted the heart, liver, lungs—and after squeezing out the excrement, they even cooked the intestines. They wasted nothing.

Sitting around the fire, we took turns grabbing pieces of meat out of a pan. It was delicious, especially after such a long day of travel.

When dinner was over, the warriors stood up, grabbed their spears, and joined the chief in leading us to their gathering area. The sky was dark. As we followed these bush experts along the path, we prayed that God would grip their hearts with the same ferocity they were gripping their spears.

"We are ready to hear your message," the chief declared.

Someone from our team proclaimed the message of the good news—from creation to the cross, explaining all Jesus had done for us . . . and them. After the message, we invited the village to follow Jesus by committing their lives to Him and laying down their traditional god and way of worship.

Many of the warriors said, "We want to believe in this Jesus you have told us about!"

Joy flooded my heart. I could hardly believe what I was witnessing. Spiritual hunger filled their souls. They immediately whirled all kinds of questions at us, such as "Why can't we see Jesus right now?" and "When will Jesus return?" and "What do we do with the god we have been worshipping," and many others.

As our discussion came to an end, the chief spoke for the group, "We want to go to all the nearby villages and share this message with everyone around us."

Before that night, this village had zero exposure to the gospel. They had never heard of Jesus. Yet as soon as they experienced the living Jesus, they were immediately compelled to tell others. The spiritual reality that infiltrated their lives was too incredible not to share. The village began living out their God-given purpose. Clearly, the Lord had chosen them as His people, and He had important assignments for them to carry out in the days ahead.

Throughout history, Christians have debated what it means that "God chooses people." More than anything, I believe these arguments reveal how we have completely missed the point. Throughout the Old Testament, God chose Israel as His people,

His special possession. What a remarkable reality as God reveals His heart and faithfulness! But I've often found myself asking, Is there more to the story? Did God choose Israel for something more than simply existing as His special people?

In Exodus 19:6 (NIV) God declares, "You will be for me a kingdom of priests and a holy nation." As a kingdom of priests, the Israelites had a God-given purpose to act as priests to all the nations, representing the one true God to every tribe on Earth. What an incredible calling! And check this out, God continues to reveal the fullness of His heart—not only for His chosen nation, Israel—but for all the nations:

> *"And* foreigners *who bind themselves to the LORD*
> *to minister to him,*
> *to love the name of the LORD,*
> *and to be his servants,*
>
> . . . .
>
> *these I will bring to my holy mountain*
> *and give them joy in my house of prayer.*
> *Their burnt offerings and sacrifices*
> *will be accepted on my altar;*
> *for* my house will be called
> a house of prayer for all nations.*"*
> *The Sovereign LORD declares—*
> he who gathers the exiles of Israel:
> *"I* will gather still others *to them*
> *besides those already gathered." (Isaiah 56:6–8 NIV,*
> *italics mine)*

GOD not only wanted the worship of Israel, He wanted the worship of every tribe, tongue, and nation! And God would use His chosen people to accomplish this vision. Simply put, God chose Israel *for* mission.

But rather than fulfilling their purpose, God's chosen people selfishly soaked in God's presence and sought out priests for themselves. They failed to proclaim His name among the nations. They failed to reveal the heart of God for every people group.

As I look around today, I'm afraid we have followed in Israel's footsteps. An evangelist friend of mine, Paul Epperson, has said, "We are the most poured into and least poured out generation!" The Israelites became spiritually fat, passive, and lazy . . . and so often the modern Church has too. God has given us as the Church the same purpose He gave Israel. He has chosen us for mission: "You are a *chosen* race, a royal priesthood, a holy nation, a people for his own possession, *that you may proclaim the excellencies of him* who called you out of darkness into his marvelous light" (1 Peter 2:9 ESV, italics mine).

Yet we have failed to accomplish the mission. How do I know this? Because we have incredible access to Christian resources on demand for our spiritual growth, as many churches to choose from as Starbucks coffee shops, paychecks with plenty of margin that could fund mission needs, armies of people who could be sent to unreached people groups—and in spite of all our tools, training and resources—we remain blind to the startling spiritual reality of the world:

61 percent of Christians have never shared their faith (Lifeway Research).

3.14 billion people (42.2 percent of the world population) live in unreached people groups (The Traveling Team Statistics).

Five out of six non-Christians in the world have no opportunity to hear the gospel (The Traveling Team Statistics).

There are 900 churches and 78,000 Evangelical Christians for every one Unreached People Group (The Traveling Team Statistics).

For every $100,000 that Christians make, they give $1 toward reaching the unreached (The Traveling Team Statistics).

Of 400,000 cross-cultural missionaries only 3 percent go to the unreached (The Traveling Team Statistics).

51 percent of church attendees in the United States were unfamiliar with the term *Great Commission* (Barna Research Group).

I can't help but imagine that, like me, you find these statistics quite staggering and eye-opening! Let's dig into them a little more deeply to discover their implications.

61 percent of Christians have never shared their faith (Lifeway Research).
It's time for us to wake up and take Jesus' commands seriously, which includes preaching the gospel to everyone (Mark 16:15). In Revelation, Jesus addresses seven churches, which many scholars believe both represents the individual local church expressions as well as the larger global Church. Jesus calls five out of those seven to repent. I wonder how much of the modern Church Jesus might be calling to repent and wake up to His commands?

3.14 billion people (42.2 percent of the world population) live in unreached people groups (The Traveling Team Statistics).
UPGs (Unreached People Groups) are ethnolinguistic groups with little to no believers, resulting in no opportunity to hear the gospel and no ability to sustain kingdom movement.

Five out of six non-Christians in the world have no

opportunity to hear the gospel (The Traveling Team Statistics).

These five out of six are not simply lost people who have rejected Jesus or live down the street from a church but choose not to go. These five out of six people in the world are those who have no opportunity to hear about Jesus, even if they wanted to. It's our job as the Church to change that.

There are 900 churches and 78,000 evangelical Christians for every one Unreached People Group (The Traveling Team Statistics).

Imagine what we could do if our churches and believers teamed up to finish the mission! Even if only one out of every 900 churches sent one out of every 78,000 believers, we would engage every remaining unreached people group. That is certainly within reach!

For every $100,000 that Christians make, they give $1 toward reaching the unreached (The Traveling Team Statistics).

This is certainly part of the problem. Where your money is, there your heart will be also. We need a heart shift!

Of 400,000 cross-cultural missionaries only 3 percent go to the unreached (The Traveling Team Statistics).

"Roughly thirty-times as many missionaries go to reached people groups to work with Christians, as go to unreached people groups. Far less go to the frontier people groups, where there are yet no believers" (R.W. Lewis).

It astounds me that so many who are called to the mission field still end up going to already reached places with well-established churches. It is not in any way bad to go to these places, but I cannot imagine that God is calling nearly all missionaries to nearly all reached places. Something needs to change.

**51 percent of church attendees in the United States
were unfamiliar with the term *Great Commission*** (Barna
Research Group).
25 percent of respondents said they heard of it but did not
recall its "exact meaning," 17 percent knew for sure, and 6
percent said they were not sure.
It's time for Jesus' final command to become our first
concern!

The alarming spiritual reality of the world and the blatant
disobedience of the Church revealed by these stunning statistics
often plague me. So I must ask: Why on Earth are we not
engaging God's mission? Why are we failing to fulfill our chosen
purpose?!

The testimony of my Pakistani friend Hamid is quite telling.
Hamid works tirelessly to see more of the world reached with the
message of Jesus. He is a true mudrunner. But he has not always
been that way. Hamid found himself evading God's mission for
many years.

"You know, Charlie," Hamid told me, "I was not a true
follower of Jesus until four years ago. Until then, I was only a
believer. I had trusted in Jesus before, but I did not really obey
what He commands us."

"What changed that for you, Hamid?" I inquired.

"I had coffee with another believer," Hamid offered, "and what
he shared with me changed my life."

"What did this man of God say to you?!" I asked. I was itching
to know.

"Well," he began, "I must first say that I have always felt I
don't have what it takes to make an impact in the world. I have
thought it's the pastors, evangelists, and leaders who are the ones
with the ability to make disciples. I am too shy to do what they
do. I am not an up-front person who can demand a crowd's attention nor am I comfortable on a stage.

"But as I met with this believer, he told me, 'Jesus does not only want pastors, evangelists, or leaders. He wants you, Hamid. He wants the everyday, common person to join Him in His mission. Jesus can use *you*! Acts 4:13 shows us that Peter and John were ordinary and uneducated men, yet they had an immense impact because they had been with Jesus. That's it. The same can be a reality for you, brother.'"

Hamid continued, "These words shattered my deepest doubts and set me free to fulfill what God has chosen me for. So I have begun to make disciples ever since. I simply invite people into my home and open God's Word with them. And many times, these people decide to follow Jesus as a result. It is exciting to see how God is working through my life!"

Hamid's testimony warmed my heart and encouraged me. "Hamid," I said, "it's amazing to hear how Jesus brought you to where you are today! It reminds me of Matthew 9:37 (ESV) where Jesus says, 'the harvest is plentiful but the laborers are few.' Jesus did not say he needed more pastors, leaders, or evangelists, as great as they are. Jesus said the greatest need in the world is more *laborers*. Laborers truly are common people found in everyday places who Jesus loves to employ—people just like you."

For years, Hamid failed to fulfill His God-given purpose because of his failures, inadequacies, and the lie he believed that kingdom impact is best left to the "experts," otherwise known as "professional Christians." Yet I was so blessed to hear how the Holy Spirit brought Hamid's life right in line with God's heart. Hamid realized that it did not matter if he had messed up too many times, didn't have the perfect words to say, didn't know every truth backward and forward, and didn't hold an influential, up-front position. None of that mattered as much as this one thing did: Jesus had chosen him for His mission!

Jesus chooses everyday people regardless of their background or shortcomings. In fact, Jesus said to each one of His imperfect, messed up, and muddied disciples, "I *chose* you and appointed you *that you should go and bear fruit*" (John 15:16 ESV, italics mine). Guess what? They too were chosen *for* mission. God chose Israel,

God chose the first twelve disciples, God chose the Maasai warriors, God chose Hamid, and God has chosen *you* too! God is in the business of choosing imperfect people for His gloriously perfect plan.

Maybe you've run from what God has called you for because you feel inadequate, ill equipped, unworthy, or imperfect. Maybe you feel that you don't know enough, that your past is too marred by sin, or that you just don't have the right words to say. Or maybe no one has ever told you about this grand mission of God and you've somehow missed seeing the vast needs of the world. Maybe you've been straight-up lazy, living a selfish, passive life. Even still, the Creator of the entire universe has chosen *you!* As believers, we are His special possession with a special purpose.

If the Lord of all has chosen us, then nothing can stop us! We have no reason to run from our purpose. We have no reason not to go. We have no reason not to share. Whatever you think is in your way, it's time—time to let go of anything that's been hindering you and time to embrace your purpose. You are chosen for mission. Your race has begun. Get up, lace your shoes, and start advancing God's kingdom—no matter the people, the place, or the cost. You are His mudrunner!

Now What?

- What has stopped you or hindered you from fully joining God's mission and ultimately fulfilling God's purposes and plans for your life?
- Read Genesis 12:3; Isaiah 49:6; Isaiah 56:6–8; Acts 9:15; and Ephesians 1:11–12. How does it feel knowing that God has chosen *you* specifically for His mission?
- For Paul the apostle to become obedient to Jesus, God had to take drastic measures. Paul was knocked down and blinded by a piercing light so that God could get his attention and say, "Hey Paul, I'm calling you to be

a light to the nations" (Acts 9:1-31). What will it take for you to pursue your purpose with passion? How will you intentionally live as a mudrunner who advances God's kingdom, no matter the people, the place, or the cost?

ADDITIONAL MISSIONS STATISTICS

According to George Barna, "A growing number of Christians don't see sharing the good news as a personal responsibility. Just 10 percent of Christians in 1993 who had shared about their faith agreed with the statement 'converting people to Christianity is the job of the local church'—as opposed to the job of an individual (i.e., themselves). Twenty-five years later, three in 10 Christians who have had a conversation about faith say evangelism is the local church's responsibility (29%), a nearly threefold increase. This jump could be the result of many factors, including poor ecclesiology (believing 'the local church' is somehow separate from the people who are a part of it) or personal and cultural barriers to sharing faith. Yet the most dramatic divergence over time is on the statement, 'Every Christian has a responsibility to share their faith.' In 1993, nine out of 10 Christians who had shared their faith agreed (89%). Today, just two-thirds say so (64%)—a 25-point drop" (www.barna.com/research/sharing-faith-increasingly-optional-christians).

Statistics from the Traveling Team

(www.thetravelingteam.org/stats)
There are 6,741 total unreached people groups.

Money and Missions:

Given to any Christian causes: $700 billion (That's also
how much we spend in America on Christmas.)

Given to Missions: $45 billion (That's only 6.4 percent of
the money given to Christian causes of any kind. That's
also how much we spend in America on dieting programs.
Embezzled: if you are doing the math and realize there is
$50 billion missing, this is where it went.)

How Christian giving is used:

- Pastoral ministries of local churches (mostly in
  Christian nations): $677 billion (96.8 percent)
- "Home Missions" in same Christian nations: $20.3
  billion (2.9 percent)
- Going to unevangelized non-Christian world: $2.1
  billion (.3 percent. This is different from the
  "unreached.")
- Money that goes toward unreached people groups
  (UPGs): estimated $450 million (In 2001 only 1
  percent of giving to "Missions" went to unreached; if
  that trend holds true today it would be $450 million.
  The estimated $450 million going toward UPGs is
  only .001 percent of the $42 trillion income of
  Christians. Americans have recently spent more money
  buying Halloween costumes for their pets than the
  amount given to reach the unreached.

Christian Workers:

Full-time Christian workers in the world: 5.5 million workers

Christian workers in the reached portions of the world: 4.19 million local workers (75.9 percent)

Christian workers in the unevangelized portions of the world: 1.3 million local workers (23.7% percent)

Christian workers in the unreached portions of the world: 20,500 local workers (0.37 percent)

Conclusions:

Evangelical Christians could provide all of the funds needed to plant a church in each of the 6,741 unreached people groups with only 0.03 percent of their income.

If every evangelical gave 10 percent of their income to missions, we could easily support 2 million new missionaries.

The Church has roughly 3,000 times the financial resources and 9,000 times the manpower needed to finish the Great Commission.

FURTHER OPPORTUNITIES
FOR YOU

CharlieMarquis.com

Check out more of what is happening in Charlie's ministry and how you can be a part of it!

Fuel For The Harvest Podcast (FuelForTheHarvest.com)

Fuel For The Harvest podcast hosts, Charlie and Nathan are coming to you from all around the world (here, there, and everywhere) with wild testimonies, tips, and talks. The mission: equipping Christians to become everyday laborers in their harvest fields (Matthew 9:35-38). It's all about living with hearts on fire and lives on purpose!

FORGE: Kingdom Building Ministries (ForgeForward.org)

Propagating a movement of more Kingdom Laborers all around the globe, anywhere and everywhere, through itinerant preaching and discipleship training focused on challenging and equipping people to fully devote their lives to

Jesus and to live lives of active ministry. Hearts on Fire. Lives on Purpose.

ForgeSpeakers.com

Check out more itinerant speakers on Charlie's ministry team! They are available to come to your event upon request.

Contact Forge:
303-745-8191
ForgeForward.org

MultiplyingMovements.com

Want to learn more about how to live practically, step-by-step a mud-running, kingdom-advancing life? Check out Forge's discipleship tool that is impacting innumerable lives all around the world: "Multiplying Movements: A Discipleship Tool for Everyday Followers of Jesus"

Ordinary people everywhere are joining God's extraordinary kingdom harvest movement. It's your turn. Are you ready to get laboring?

NOTES

20. Chasing Wanderers

1. *Hacksaw Ridge*, directed by Mel Gibson, written by Robert Schenkkan and Andrew Knight (Santa Monica, CA: Lionsgate, 2016).

29. The Humble Exalted

1. Free Burma Rangers, directed by Brent Gudgel and Chris Sinclair, written by Brent Gudgel (Austin, TX: Deidox Films; Nashville, TN: Lifeway, 2020).

ABOUT THE AUTHOR

Charlie Marquis has always had a knack for mischief and adventure. Growing up, he often found himself taking on the role of pranking mastermind, rallying the troops for trouble.

Yet when Jesus gripped his life, everything changed.

Charlie's insatiable craving for mischievous ventures never left. Instead, it transformed into a passion for kingdom troublemaking: proclaiming the gospel in as many places as possible—here, there, and everywhere—even if it's prohibited or deemed "too dangerous."

Charlie is passionate about seeing the kingdom of God advanced among the unreached, unengaged, and frontier regions of the world. Charlie's heartbeat is "to preach the gospel where Christ [is] not known" (Romans 15:20 NIV). So he has put his feet to his faith, traveling extensively to unreached people groups across the globe.

When not venturing into remote mission fields, Charlie travels from place to place, preaching everywhere for all sorts of events. Speaking with intensity and urgency, he shares captivating God stories, passionately challenging crowds to give everything to Jesus and engage in God's everyday mission—whether across the street or across the sea.

When not traveling, Charlie lives in Colorado along with his incredible wife and family.

Want to invite Charlie to speak at your event or explore his ministry? Visit CharlieMarquis.com.